The Greater World of Little Things

The Greater World of Little Things

Ross Gardner

Brambleby Books

The Greater World of Little Things
Copyright © Ross Gardner 2016

The author has asserted his right
under the Copyright, Designs and Patents Act 1988
to be identified as the Author of this Work.

All Rights Reserved
No part of this book may be reproduced in any form
by photocopying or by any electronic or mechanical means,
including information, storage or retrieval systems,
without permission in writing from both the copyright
owner and the publisher of this book.

A CIP catalogue record for this book is available
from the British Library

ISBN 978 1908241 382

Cover design by Tanya Warren – Creatix
Cover image by the author

First published in 2016 by BRAMBLEBY BOOKS,

www.bramblebybooks.co.uk

Printed by CreateSpace, an Amazon.com Company

Dedication

For Lola – ever an inspiration.

About the Author

Ross Gardner was born near Southend in Essex and for as long as he can remember has held a great affinity for the natural world. With a childhood spent experiencing the wild wonders of his local woods, grassland and marshes, this developed over the years into a deeply felt passion. Having gained a degree in Rural Environmental Management, he has since enjoyed the good fortune of being able to unite a lifetime's interest with his professional life, first as manager of a nature study centre and then as a member of the education department at a country park, both located not far from where he has grown up in South Essex. With both, he has continually been able to enjoy the privilege of imparting his knowledge and love of nature with the young people and others. As a self-confessed generalist, it is the sheer variety in nature, rather than in any one group, that captivates him so overwhelmingly. It is through this that he has found himself turning to the written word as a means of expressing his passions, having penned several books and numerous articles.

Foreword

On the street where I live nature each year breaks out from the least cracks between paving stones, the lea of garden walls, the edges of the car park and from recesses in the long stretch of a Roman wall that our council sees fit to hide behind said car park, as if it were an embarrassing remnant of life before the internal combustion engine. In spring, this 'nature' takes the form of carpets of crucifers, bittercress, whitlow grass, shepherd's purse, and, in a few small places on the Roman wall, the scarce rue-leaved saxifrage. Then, in succession, come dandelions, groundsel, ragwort, daisies, knotgrass, wall-flower, creeping thistle, willowherbs, mallow, ox-tongue, and a host of other plants, providing nectar and pollen for bees and hoverflies, and both seeds and insect-food for our treasured local populations of house-sparrows, tits, blackbirds, robins and swifts.

This is one of those often overlooked places whose praises are sung in this book's advocacy of the 'small things' with whom we share our lives, and on whom we depend, whether we are aware of it or not. Ross Gardner's book refers often to the writings of others – especially the nature-writers of a hundred or more years ago – and its author is evidently aware of the scientific literature. More than anything, however, it is the work of someone with a deep, direct and powerfully experienced connection with the natural world and its inhabitants. On second thoughts, however, this phrase 'natural world' is very misleading – it fails to capture one of the central themes of the book: interconnectedness. Gardner begins with a fine, detailed description of a favourite spot by a stretch of railway line – the hedgerow ash trees, the small mammal burrows in the soil below, the visiting bumblebees and butterflies, attracted by the wayside flowers, and his first chiff-chaff of the spring. Gardner traces the closely observed interconnections between these animals, plants and their physical location, much in the spirit of Darwin's famous account of his 'tangled bank'.

Part of the point of this is to indicate a certain shift from our initial impressions of a place, powerful as these may be, to a closer, more intimate appreciation of the complexity of interdependencies, webs, networks that link together the many inhabitants of an apparently undistinguished spot. But, never far from Gardner's thoughts in his descriptive passages is a consciousness of his own presence as both part of and apart from the scenes he describes. This is a second persistent thread that runs through the book. How are we to understand ourselves in relation to the countless other species that surround us? There are passages where Gardner reminds us of the destructiveness of industrialised agriculture and of the wider, global threats of climate change and loss of biodiversity. He engages, too, with the controversy surrounding Lovelock's idea of 'gaia', and the possibility that the earth as a self-regulating system has a history that parallels the micro-level interactions that are characterised by the idea of natural selection.

These speculations are not, however, central to Gardner's message in this book. They are the backdrop to his much more frequent image of a single, sensitive and perceptive observer, trying to make sense of her or his immediate surroundings. Even in saying this, I risk misrepresentation. Part two of the book is about changing perspectives. Through a series of chapters, Gardner seeks to extend, even displace the centrality of the subjective place from which the observer sees. One intriguing chapter explains how a three-year survey of bumblebees in the environmental centre where he worked enabled him not quite to experience the world as a bumblebee might experience it. The sequence of flowers through the season, offering, in turn, pollen and nectar required by the bees and their brood, the different niches where these flowers could be sought, the other insects that compete with the bees for these 'rewards', the mammals and birds whose activities crisscross the foraging routes of the bees, the 'cuckoo' bumblebees that seek out the nests of their more industrious relatives – all of these, and the vicissitudes of weather, too, come into a newly perceived set of relations when viewed through the perspective of the lives of the bees.

Ted Benton

Naturalist and author

Contents

Introduction	13
The World of Little Things	13
Look and Look Again	14
Part 1. Remembering How to Look	19
Remembering How to Look	20
Extraordinarily Ordinary	28
The Lay of the Land	44
The Pool: a lesson in looking	63
Part 2: Shifting Perspectives	69
Shifting Perspectives	70
A Bumblebee's Eye View	77
The World Afloat	92
Middle Ground?	100
Part 3: Common Ground	109
Common Ground	110
Human Needs	125
Part 4: The Meaning of Things	145
Simple Nature	146
The Meaning of Things	147
Different Folks…	169
Acknowledgements	172
Bibliography	173
Species mentioned in text	177

Introduction

The World of Little Things

The world of little things is vast indeed.
So big we mostly never see it, as
It slithers and threads, and scurries, and crawls.
Creeps lightly, springs swift, and wanders its weave.

Its noise never stops – a murmur beyond
Our listening, so often gone unheard,
While it whispers and wings, sustains and sings.
Treads deftly, swims stealth, and layers its throng.

It lives between things and underneath things.
There are those that grow on others – others
That grow on them, and there are the strands that
Bind together the others in between.

It moves on legs by the dozen, or none
Whatsoever, or by a leap of faith,
Or with the gift of blissful ignorance,
Or satisfaction of a job well done.

It feeds on everything and nothing:
Things unspeakable and nature's purest.
Thrives on labour, the essence of being.
Vast indeed, is this world of little things.

(Poem by author)

Look and Look Again

With nature, as with so many other facets of our engagement with the world, first impressions are important. They are borne from the subconscious, from the instinctive self. Even though the importance of nature in our lives may be difficult to express, there is that deep-seated, unspoken and indeed instinctive sense of its value and worth. We go on to be shaped by our experiences and it is they that continue to resonate and ring true. But conversely and somewhat contradictorily, they are also insufficient. It can safely be said and without the slightest delusion towards any sort of profundity, that nature is big, much bigger than the spaces we would normally expect it to occupy. While those initial impressions of it are powerful and significant, they could never reveal all that might feasibly be revealed. Besides those simple pleasures that can be enjoyed without effort, this too is one of the greatest wonders of the natural world.

If indeed we are fortunate enough to find ourselves in such circumstances that allow us the time and opportunity to reflect on the externalities of our relationship with nature and the many and various benefits that this can bring, it is a similar contradiction that comes into play. That of achieving a balance between not crowding out those 'simple pleasures' with the unnecessary complication that would make them unattainable, and applying the sufficient scrutiny of those things that inspire and enthral. It is this that I hope this book achieves in appropriate measure.

A second impression is required – a third, a fourth, and more. Through my work in environmental education, I have been able to impart with many young people some of the knowledge that I have gleaned from my passion for nature that has been with me for most of my years. The importance for increasing the awareness of nature to anybody, young or old, cannot be stated too highly. Open the eyes of even just a couple of people, and they might do the same with two more each. Those four could become eight, then sixteen… and so begins a quiet revolution.

From a personal point of view, I have also been given ample opportunity to see things that have become so very familiar to me, with something of that thrill of newness and wonder that I have been able to see in young eyes genuinely amazed at witnessing remarkable things for the first time; vicariously revisiting the same, fresh fascination that I experienced in my own childhood. I may look more purposefully at the little wolf spider scurrying to safety with her bundle of eggs attached to the tip of her abdomen. I might take the time to admire the cheerful beauty of the Ox-eye Daisy flower among the grasses and I am freshly impressed by the wonderfully gaudy and unmoth-like burnet moths with their dazzling red spots on dark metallic green. It is easy to forget sometimes just how exquisite a Small White butterfly is, rather than just another 'cabbage white', how truly outlandish a bush-cricket can look, or how deep the intrigue of the weedy depths of some unassuming looking pool. And how do they all share the spaces of the places in which they live? What other tiny legs tread, along with those of the wolf spider, among the towering mass of the grasses; what else vies for space alongside the sun-smiling daisies; what other wings are over-looked, beyond the shining colours of the unlikely looking moths? How, indeed, does each and every one of these living things combine to paint a perfect picture? I have gathered what some might regard as a considerable amount of natural history knowledge over the years, but I am delighted to admit that I have missed more than I have acquired.

The reasons for such intrigue, such fascination and admiration, such deeply felt significance may therefore present us with matters for a great deal of consideration. They are questions that can be difficult to grasp and yet at the same time might require only a bit more looking – really looking – to trigger the necessary chain of thought. It may provide a challenge of the imagination and the notions of our own place within it all. For those who refute the idea of the separateness of the human race from the rest of life and seek in some way to redress our remoteness from it, we ourselves might be regarded as yet another of its contradictions. Assuming that we are secure in our lives, we will always tend towards a view of nature from our own anthropocentric perspective and yet yearn to consciously be an integral part of it. Our powers of reflection and highly developed sense of 'self' will always make our reconciling of these notions a challenge, but one to be met and cherished and which would further a sense of value for nature, beyond even the realms of our direct contact with it.

To leave aside for a moment such philosophising and hopefully dispel any esoteric pretensions, it has become increasingly evident to me, as already mentioned, that such inquiry should just as much be directed towards the familiar things as to our more obviously remarkable experiences. As detailed in her *Ecology of a Garden*, Dr Jennifer Owen recorded more than 2,000 species of plant and animal in her normal, suburban Leicester garden, persuading her to conclude that it (along with, she supposed, other gardens in general) included "*an astonishingly large proportion of the species recorded in the British Isles.*" This is a notion that few would give credit to, myself included, until the detail of the facts are explained. Even if we don't have at our disposal the expertise to identify 550 species of parasitic wasp (and let's face it, there are very few around who would!), 340 species of moth, or the means to identify 60-plus kinds of spider, the message is a clear one and applicable to anywhere that we have come to think we know very well.

It is within such things and their domestic environs where the first inklings of wildness are to be found, yet so often ignored and unnoticed. It is an understated but true wildness that begins to further unfold as soon as we set foot outside the front gate in renewed search of the woods and fields, seashores and marshes that we thought we knew well, and could know better, a wildness that might seem improbable to some. Maybe it is something I look too hard for. It is possible that a wistful longing allows me to see what I hope to find rather than what is really there. But perhaps I…we do need to be more attentive to it – so much has changed. I think of my own home ground. There are more car parks and buildings sprawled across some of those little corners where nature found its niches, amid what I remember as a kind of ambling suburbia, when Sundays were proper Sundays, quieter and more pensive. Even the open spaces that remain (of which, I am pleased to say, many still do) must bear the increasing weight of the growing pressures of changing times. Such places where nature may still express itself more completely must be experienced to their fullest and those experiences explored more deeply. It is this that offers hope for the future.

There follows then a consideration, or should I say a reconsideration, of the things, the places and ideas that might bring us closer to that big world of little things. Of thoughts pertaining to something of re-evaluation of the big things in the eye and mind of the individual and of the small things as part of the bigger picture. A contemplation of the frivolous and the fundamental; the apparently obvious and seemingly unremarkable; of places and perspective. A collection, I suppose, of essays that I think would stand alone in their own right, but also strung, however loosely, about that common theme. As for setting such ideas into words, it is another challenge. I guess I could at times be accused of taking something of a romantic stance in my efforts to do so. The experiences herein are genuine and attainable and hopefully, during the more philosophical moments, the reasoning sound. The words are sincere and, in my own mind at least, I have attempted to place these thoughts into the context of the stern challenges that face the world of nature and us with it.

Romantic perhaps, but not idealised. Surely I'm not the only one to sometimes feel, when enthralled by the wild and windswept landscapes or equally when enveloped by the defiant layers of life thriving within some embattled bastion of urban greenery, that a small part of me is somewhere else. The same physical location, of course, but somehow more distant, embroiled more deeply within the ageless layers of nature's persistence. A construct of the mind no doubt, but enough to wonder, to look and imagine.

Part 1

Remembering How to Look

Remembering How to Look

One of the ever expanding joys of observing nature and something that has become increasingly significant to me over the years is the constant surprise, the perpetuation of interest, the sheer wonder of life's variety that may be present in nearly any situation, in spite of the continued degradation and human pressures put upon it. It is something that may be as relevant in those places where nature's riches are very evident, as much as it is in circumstances where the presence of wild things is a genuine surprise. For every Raven that tumbles above the lower mountain slopes, millions of tiny feet tread near soundlessly among the heather and moorland grass below, and for each set of gliding wings of butterflies skimming across the woodland glade thousands more fly in their wake barely noticed. And for every probing beak along the winter coast there will be countless quantities of mud-dwelling snails and shrimps, while among the scattered riches of the herb-rich downland slopes, the buzz, the scurry, the flit all emanate prolifically from flowery acres.

As for those more surprising circumstances, their intrigue is no less considerable. There is a spot by a railway line in Essex where I have had cause, on occasion, to stop and look. A gate beside a lay-by along a lane, where railway workers park and gain access to the line for maintenance work. In most respects, such could be encountered along many a lane, in many a county. It is probably, however, not a spot where one might normally pause and observe. If it wasn't for the fact that it provided a convenient place to meet some of the local school children who walked cross-country from their school to the nature study centre where I worked recently, I doubt I would ever have done so. Yet it is here in early spring that I have stood and listened to the first – to me – Chiffchaff of the year calling from the Ash trees beside the railway line or before but not equated it with a reason to break from our walk, Jefferies unravels the dappled and largely hidden world of the hedgerow. He tells us of nothing that we would be surprised to know was there, but makes us think of them, for want of a better phrase, in a more 'joined-up' way.

The reason for the tiny avalanche of earth is the fall of a single mouse's foot. One of the resident rodents that has threaded the bank with unseen trails and leafy tunnels, "*no broader than a ribbon*" and that run beneath the Herb-robert and Ground Ivy, dock and nettle leaves that crowd the slope of the mound in the summer. With this inexorable erosion of the bank by teeth and feet, and even the meagre thimblefuls of soil inadvertently dislodged and over time accumulating to affect the movement of water in the ditch below, it is the mice, he says, that "*represent in living shape the yet slower and unseen, but ceaseless attrition of non-animate forces.*" And he considers the notion of the networks of little pathways and tunnels irrigating the soil, carrying water into the mound and down to the roots, furthering the growth of hedgerow trees and shrubs. The mice are no longer just mice, but agents of change, very subtle, but change nonetheless. And not only the mice but also the 'humblebees' and wasps that he says "*excavate far more than would be supposed*", and the water rats (voles) that swim in the water of the ditch at the foot of the mound and make their burrows in the bank.

Here is a hedgerow, with the description of its creatures and plants, the passage of water and the physical stuff of the bank on which it stands, where nothing is to be considered in isolation and with each component of it given equal regard. The feather-light touches of insects and the not quite soundless caress of the wayside animals carrying as much significance as the leaf-laden branches and boughs rising above the ground and the roots of trees and shrubs that shape the very profile of the bank and hedge.

enjoyed the first of those late-March, vernal rays warming this unlikely heat trap. A Great-spotted Woodpecker might bounce, chirping loudly over head towards a nearby group of oak trees, and butterflies can be seen in the summer skipping along this sunny, undisturbed (by people if not by trains) ribbon of land. These, though, are the more obvious natural attributes of this stretch of railway line. I have long appreciated the 'green corridor' qualities of railway lines, especially in built-up areas or where, as often the case, areas of wildlife habitat are effectively islands cast adrift amid an arable sea. These things are important but do not provide the crux of what is being considered here.

It is one of those situations that perhaps reminds us 'how to look'. Not always is it necessary to focus down into the nooks and crannies to absorb the essence of a place. The ambience of a foaming upland river should wash over our senses as its water does the boulders in its course. There are times when one can only stand in awe and wonder at the outrageous mountain country of northern Scotland. But there are those instances when the fine detail does indeed unfold a world of breadth and wonder of a different kind.

When watching over the comings and goings of life beside the railway, there was another observer that I would often call to mind. With an uncanny ability to see – to sense – the smallest facet of place and time, Richard Jefferies' (1848-87) keenly honed faculty of observation could, with seemingly uneventful instances, enliven within the imagination a world brocaded with layers of fresh detail. Not necessarily just in terms of simple details but also by way of considering what we already see, hear and feel in a different way. In an essay entitled *Hedge Miners*, written in 1881 (see Jefferies, 1948), he casts such an alternative light as this upon an ordinary country hedgerow. The mound of his hedge-bank is excavated and shaped by "*the least of creatures.*" From the sprinkling of a thimbleful of soil that rustles through the foliage, something we all will have heard

Back by the railway line and the same notions of that writer, expressed so eloquently more than a hundred years previously, can still be applied. While the Chiffchaff and others are so very gratefully received, it is such things as the track-side 'weeds', squeezing up between the ballast scree that has tumbled from the endless snaking ridge, that begin to push the message more forcefully into view. The yellow sprinkling of Hawk's-beard flowers that most passing by might be unlikely to note, and the rosettes of Plantains – the oval leaves of the Greater and the lanceolate ones of the Ribwort species – pressed against the stones. The obligatory and barely heeded stand of Stinging Nettle crowded beside the concrete gate post and the selection of grasses that have gained a toehold – the brome, bent and meadow-grasses. Thus, the platform is set which is in effect a micro-world of niches and opportunities to be filled, just as it is any wood or meadow, although here their unfolding is perhaps rather less likely to be a matter of observation than in either of those places.

The potential of the highways and byways, roadsides and waysides as a sanctuary for beleaguered wildlife is indeed everywhere to be seen. By way of example, the better vegetated sections of this length of track are inhabited by Adders, which favour the south-facing embankment and its warmth in the early spring sunshine. Moreover, I would imagine that most of us have watched from the car the Kestrel hovering over the road-side verges, while Knapweed and Ox-eye Daisy seem to have an increasing presence over the grassy areas at the side of the motorways and A roads; a most pleasant distraction during those all too frequent traffic jams when the usual view is of the back end of the car in front.

The 'Roadside Nature Reserve' is a concept of modern conservation; an indictment of the extent to which some of our wild plants and animals have been squeezed over recent decades. These are now the frontiers where the likes of Sulphur Clover and Crested Cow-wheat can thrive among the intensively cultivated boulder clay-fields of East Anglia. Where the Chalkhill Blue might flutter along a Kentish lane, in search of the Horseshoe Vetch on which to lay its eggs, and where Stinking Hellebore and Lady Orchid flowered before they flew. It was in Kent when an elusive public footpath sign resulted in my confronting by a busy A road. Not an ideal location for a peaceful country walk and not in this instance home to scarce and beautiful orchids, but its every step was enlivened by the busy flight of Small Skipper butterflies among a verdant sward and the inky gloss of Six-spot Burnet moths scattered about the flower heads of Yarrow, Knapweed and Red Clover.

Where intensive farming and development have left some species in such a parlous state, the roadside verge offers for some species something of a final sanctuary and often a vital corridor between isolated areas of wildlife habitat. A mere green blur seen outside the car window they most certainly are not. For even without the more unusual, the springtime stands of Hedge-garlic and the summery music of the grasshoppers in the sward are always a welcome pleasure. And even without containing any of those rarities found elsewhere, such communities may nevertheless prove remarkable. It was just this point, of course, that Jefferies fully understood. What other little corners of the countryside are there, full of treasures yet undiscovered.

The plants that grow along the aforementioned length of railway line are not rare as such, but each provides sustenance or shelter for some creature or other. Along the 30 or so metre length between the lay-by and the road that passes the head of the lane, some 30 species of flowering plants can be seen. The oak, Horse Chestnut and willow that shade the verges. The Wood Avens, Red Campion and Cuckoo-pint growing in the lea of the trees. The clover and buttercup that take advantage of the sunny breaks in the leaf-shade above, and the Hawthorn and Elder that colour the spaces in-between.

There are to be found Jefferies' *"non-animate forces"* a plenty; not so much 'Hedge Miners' as 'Railway Workers'. Rodents in number, I am quite sure (although I have never seen them), running their trails through the undergrowth; not Water Voles through lack of habitat, but certainly the Bank Vole and Wood Mouse that I know inhabit the hedgerows hereabouts. As for the small creatures that bring their little influences to bear on the place, the Ringlet and Small White butterflies that flutter about the nearby Bramble blossom will doubtlessly be noticed by others that walk along the lane in late spring, so too the tireless labours of the bumblebees and the steady buzzing of large hoverflies just above their heads.

I have come to know the Brambles that grow along the lane well. One spring and summer I watched and noted the ebb and flow of life among one particular, unremarkable tangle of thorny stems, scrambling for six or seven metres beside the lane and barely extending more than a couple of metres away from the verge. I could see that this labyrinthine bundle of prickle-ridden, trailing branches supported an assemblage of wild creatures of great density and diversity, with each offering its own insight into nature's propensity for filling in gaps, with no niche left unoccupied, no resource left unexploited. Aristotle nearly two and half millennia ago supposed that *"nature abhors a vacuum"*. He might not have intended this theory to be applied in such an ecological context as this, but they are words that often come into my head when I find myself marvelling at the frequently astonishing variety of wild creatures inhabiting unlikely corners in unlikely places.

No others illustrate this better than the caterpillars of a tiny leaf-mining moth by the name of *Stigmella aurella*. An adult would barely measure four millimetres in length and its larvae are so small as to be able to feed inside a bramble leaf, tattooing its surface with the twisting pattern of the 'mine' whilst leaving the structure of the leaf intact. Along with the moth, I found and identified nearly 40 different invertebrate species, just through casual observation alone. How many more a beating tray or night-time visits would have added I can only guess, but it would very likely have at least doubled the final figure. In the day it was not only butterflies, bees and the attention seeking hoverflies that could be found but also the leaf-green Speckled Bush-crickets and the terminally patient spiders, suspended in their orbs. There were ichneumon wasps seeking out the caterpillars and other larvae undoubtedly present beyond the limits of my own sight and Soldier Beetles that came to prey on the other smaller species that defied my identification.

These are all the 'lesser creatures', the movers of soil and substrate that a passer-by along the lane could very well miss: ants scouring the nettle stems for aphids (greenfly), 'farmed' for their honeydew and that search among the ballast for any morsel to be taken back to the nest; a tiny, sinuous rove beetle – perhaps a devourer of algae or scavenger of organic detritus – shiny black but for the red 'saddle' of its thorax, beads itself between the spaces among the stones, without daring to stray too far from the cool shade of the overhanging vegetation; and a little digger wasp that flies deliberately and ominously as it searches the foliage for insects with which to stock its burrows as live, but paralysed, food for its young. Other, much smaller hoverflies – *Platycheirus* or *Melonastoma* – hardly more than a millimetre wide and barely a centimetre and half long (species more for the hoverfly enthusiast perhaps), 'nose about' the Hawk's-beard and dead-nettle flowers. And how many see the little *Pardosa* wolf spiders scrambling across the embankment slope, to bask in the heat perhaps, or to take sustenance from other small creatures unwary of this fast moving predator in their midst?

From this web of life quietly threading among the weeds and the ballast, who knows what goes on under the cover of a dark night, or indeed, who would be passing and inclined to stop and look? By day, the scurries of small mammals, the moths disturbed from their cover, the gangly limbed bush-crickets clambering among the shrubby plants offer an inkling. Once, whilst peering among the litter accumulating beneath the bramble scrub, my eyes caught sight of a snail shell and a glow-worm larva feasting on the increasingly former occupant. All are aspects of this nocturnal world, transformed from the unassuming leaves and branches of the day. And all of this need not be attributed to the vast and corporeal darkness of the deep forest, as well it might, but rather to thoughts that emerge from observing a lay-by, next to a railway line, along a leafy Essex lane.

Extraordinarily Ordinary

Jefferies' hedgerow reminds us of the dense weft of life that often lies woven beneath the shawl of familiarity and apparent mundanity of our everyday places, places that may stir a desire within us to examine them anew and be surprised at what we find. While we may more readily appreciate the potential for that often ignored length of hedgerow to harbour the stuff of such amazement, in other instances the situation can be a most unlikely one and our focus within it no less improbable.

In this light, I imagine that most would agree that the potholed car park of a large town football ground is a decidedly unexpected location to experience a sudden flash of awareness of these ubiquitous qualities of nature. To be reminded of how much we normally miss of our world, even as it passes clear within our sight, but only through the peripheral vision of the mind's eye. An odd place to experience, it might be said, a minor epiphany an epiphany because it concerned the Feral Pigeon, one of the more scorned and certainly most ignored members of our country's (and that of many others) bird fauna. It is probably fair to say that the pigeon is not a true image of nature to most people.

As far as the inspiration for such a chapter in a book is concerned, it need not have been about pigeons at all. There are various other close 'neighbours' to chose from, but for that particular moment of inspiration that sets the mind in motion along a certain track, it was indeed a humble pigeon. While later, considering this very idea, I caught sight of a silver-fish scuttling away to safety from the glare of the light that I had rudely flooded the bathroom with. Whilst possessing a certain degree of pest potential with a diet of starchy materials, such as paper, fabrics and even glue, I found them to be quite fascinating little creatures, with a complex mating ritual, their own place in a 'domestic' ecosystem and a lifespan upwards of two years. What's more, they belong to an immensely old Order of insects that arose during the early dawn of insect evolution more than 400 million years ago. Plenty of material, I am sure, with which to fill a chapter's worth of pages.

There would be other contenders for triggering novel thoughts about nature. Most houses have their communities of spiders in one form or another, great dividers of opinion, but in equal measure, wonderful exemplars of adaptation and ingenuity. The all too familiar, hairy-legged House Spider, with a scurry across the carpet to shiver a spine but possessing everything that makes spiders such an intriguing groups of animals. Or the gangly limbed Daddy-long-legs Spider, loping silently within the recesses underneath bookshelves and behind radiators. In our gardens the list of candidates would be a long one; the centipedes hunting under the stones and logs; the ants under the lawn – indeed, any of the array of common place creatures that live their quiet and not so quiet lives in our little patches of flowery green.

But, as it turned out, pigeons it was to be. They are in many ways the perfect analogue for the ignored and the reviled, the invisibly familiar or the infuriatingly obvious. And to a few they might provide a precious fragment of the wild into the inner-city heartlands or, indeed, a surprising insight into the persistence of nature. The birds and their place in the urban ecology with its own unique labyrinth of city-hardy life cycles and interactions reveal as much as any of the hidden wonder of the mundane.

There can be few in the UK that have at some point visited a large town or city that are not familiar with the Feral Pigeon. Only perhaps in our disaffection for them could we refer to them at all as 'lesser creatures', such is their obviousness as a part of urban life. It is to the Normans that we must look to for their origins in Britain, having brought them from the continent as dovecote birds, kept as a supply of fresh meat. The Royal Society for the Protection of Birds put the British population at least 1,000 breeding pairs, concentrated mainly around the larger urban centres. The population in Europe as a whole (including the ancestral – and now scarce in Britain – Rock Dove) has been estimated at somewhere between 18 and 23 million birds. Estimations for city pigeon populations appear to be surprisingly few and far between, although one study published in the *Canadian Journal of Zoology* put the number of Feral Pigeons at large in Milan at the turn of this century at a whopping 103,000, whereas Sheffield is thought to boast a mere 12,000. With 20,000-40,000 birds thought to be present in the 1960s, the London population may well be somewhere in the middle.

Further afield, the Feral Pigeon is of trans-continental renown, absent only from the Earth's polar extremes. It seems that wherever they are, their presence can polarise opinion. From those who feed them and delight in their company to those that bemoan the mess made by their droppings and claim them to be feathered purveyors of disease – proverbial 'winged rats'. While there are those who would cite a proven risk from pathogens contained in pigeon faeces to human health, it has been asserted (in this instance by the UK-based Pigeon Control Resource Centre) that such dangers are something of a myth perpetuated for gain by the media wishing to sell newspapers and the pest control industry endeavouring to sell its services – *"the likelihood of a human being contracting a disease from contact with pigeons or their excrement is virtually nil."*

I must admit that even I, who endeavours to view the natural world through as objective a pair of eyes as possible, had never previously regarded the Feral Pigeon as quite the same as other birds. Well, it's not really a wild bird, is it? They may have originally descended from the native Rock Dove, but they are practically tame and hardly ever seen away from towns and cities. I, like many other people, relate them more with the high street than the countryside. But where does this leave the

Canada Goose or Ring-necked Parakeet, two non-natives to have established feral/wild populations via accidental introductions in the UK? The latter species is an Indian native now thought to have a breeding population of maybe as many as than 8600 pairs that has grown since a comparatively recent introduction in the middle of the 20th century. The geese are very much associated with urban lakes and reservoirs whilst the parakeets are known chiefly from London and the suburban fringes of the Home Counties. They are scarcely, if at all, more 'wild' than the Feral Pigeons that have to look after themselves to just the same extent. Arguably the only real difference are the more 'exotic' origins of the other two in terms of their indigenous ranges. Yet we are generally (although I have heard of birdwatchers that do despise the Canada Goose) much more ready to accept them as part of our perception of 'wild Britain', an inconsistency that I too confess to being guilty of. Even the wild Rock Doves might not be quite as wild as we would like to think. A paper written in 1966 by R.K. Murton and N.J. Westwood claimed that because of our long association with pigeons, which goes back thousands of years, and the cycle of domestication and escape back into wild carried out many times "*it would be most unlikely that the purity of wild populations has remained unaffected anywhere in the range of the species.*" The boundaries then are further blurred.

As for the 'wild' Rock Dove, their UK distribution is now limited to the northern and western coasts of Scotland and coastal Northern Ireland. Without close human proximity, they choose to nest on rock ledges and cliffs. It is this desire that is accommodated by the buildings of human settlement, allowing their feral descendants to become such a familiar part of the urban scene. Of the "*small rounded bodies upon the cornice*" of the British Museum, Richard Jefferies observed in his book *The Life of the Fields*: "*To them the building is merely a rock, pierced with convenient caverns; they use its exterior for their purpose, but penetrate no farther.*" What then do we think we mean by 'wild'?

With a Tuesday afternoon to spare, I had arrived at Roots Hall, the home ground of Southend United Football Club, to watch a reserve match (the sort of football you really do need to be at a loose end to think about watching). In spite of my previously dismissive attitudes towards them, this is a location I have long associated with the Feral Pigeon, albeit indirectly. They are ever-present inside the ground on match days, swooping in and out of the roof rafters of the ageing stands, causing anyone sitting beneath them to glance up nervously for fear of a surprise 'gift' from above. I had even once watched a small group being chased over the roof of the opposite stand by a Peregrine Falcon. One had just crapped liberally across my father's knee and we convinced ourselves that it was the culprit that was set to become the falcon's next meal!

The Peregrine provides an interesting sub-plot to the story of the Feral Pigeon's place within the ecosystem of the city. Although it seems likely that the Peregrine's diet will be determined to a large degree by the relative abundances of available prey, they and the pigeon are often viewed as traditional opposites in the predator-prey divide. In urban localities this is very likely to prove the case. Far from being widely regarded as a townie, the Peregrine is a bird more readily associated with upland habitats and coastal cliffs, where, like the Rock Dove/Feral Pigeon, they usually seek out some rocky ledge on which to nest. A Peregrine is a supremely powerful aerial predator, more so than its fellow British falcons: the lithesome Hobby, the agile Kestrel and the fleet-winged little Merlin. They will eat a variety of medium-sized birds (along with the occasional small mammal and even an earthworm or two!). During wintertime they will often frequent coastal marshes, where the first evidence of their presence might be a frenzied explosion of wings filling the air, with roosting or feeding waders alarmed *en masse* by a sudden ambush. The calm that follows the chaos is interrupted only by the blinking, laser-yellow eye of the hunter as it stands over the unfortunate plover or sandpiper gripped in its talons. J.A. Baker's (1967) famous Peregrines sampled such varied fare as Black-headed Gulls, Fieldfare, Moorhen, Curlew and Rook, whilst those nesting on Exeter Cathedral and using the city's lights to hunt at night even catch such rarities as migrating Corn Crakes.

The pigeon in many situations is perhaps something of a favourite (Baker's birds took a great many Woodpigeon), but they are no slouches themselves and no easy catch for a predator. Their own ability to attain speeds that approach 80 kilometres per hour during level flight requires a similar feat of aerial swiftness on the part of the Peregrine. Indeed, the Peregrine's speed is unsurpassed among all birds. In level flight they can outstrip a pigeon, having been recorded, exceptionally, achieving speeds of more than 90 kilometres per hour. While stooping however – plummeting, from on high, in for the kill – they can move through the air at an astonishing and devastating 320 kilometres per hour, perhaps even more. The falcon's bill is in theory deployed to deliver the decisive, fatal blow, but the sheer ferocity of impact must surely do the job on most occasions. As fast moving as the pigeon is, it is the ready food supply and abundance of satisfactory alternative nesting habitat that has advanced the Peregrines' seemingly unlikely appearance in cities across the UK.

Just as much as we are reminded by the Peregrine of nature's tenacity and regenerative potential, its fortunes also recall the human potential for effortless and far-reaching catastrophe. To remember their plight back in the 1960s, their presence in our most built-up, industrialised areas seems all the more unlikely still. As a consequence of the use of DDT in the 1950s and '60s, numbers fell to less than 400 individual birds. This presumed safe chemical pesticide, used so widely during the mid-20th century, persisted and accumulated in the food chain. For top predators, like the Peregrine, levels of the chemical resulted in a drastic crash in numbers, due in a large part to broods lost through the premature cracking of their egg shells, which had thinned as a result of DDT poisoning. The use of the pesticide was subsequently phased out, and numbers, along with other birds of prey, began to increase. In spite of continued persecution from gamekeepers and pigeon fanciers, the British population has risen to a rather less precarious 1,400. This is an increase that has seen them appearing in many of our cities and larger towns, such as Bristol and London in the south, Birmingham and Derby in the Midlands, and Manchester and Liverpool in the north. Some of the London birds are perhaps the most well known, given their choice of high profile nesting sites, not least the Tate Modern and the Houses of Parliament!

With thoughts of any kind of birdwatching far from my mind, I had arrived at the football ground somewhat early and decided to stay in the car and read the news paper for a short while rather than sit around in a draughty old football stadium (reserve games – perhaps unsurprisingly – do not attract much of a crowd at Southend). Taking a moment to look up from the paper, my attention was drawn by a brief flapping of wings. I looked to find a pair of pigeons 15 metres or so from the car and found myself watching their antics with a growing attentiveness. Even though at the time I knew relatively little about the courtship behaviour of pigeons, it was obvious that they were male and female. The would-be suitor was strutting around his intended partner, with his chest feathers puffed out to make the most of the gleaming, iridescent green feathers around his neck. She was resisting his overtures, jerking hurriedly away, but he persisted. Another male fluttered down to try his luck but didn't get any further than a brief, posturing confrontation with the other. The challenger seen off, the original male returned to his courtship pursuits. I must have seen this small drama acted out on numerous occasions before but only now did I find myself momentarily captivated by it.

The full gamut of pigeon courtship will also involve much bowing, fanning of the tail feathers and soft 'cooing'. The behaviour of the male and female, culminating with their beaks being held together, completes that well-known idiom to 'bill and coo', as a display of the affectionate attentions of lovers. Despite their unfavourable reputation, the behaviour and natural history of the Feral Pigeon has actually received a great deal of research and not only from those who might seek to eradicate or control them. Various books have been written on the subject, not least Richard Johnston and Marián Janiga's book *Feral Pigeons*, an in-depth scientific exploration of the birds and also, it would seem, something of a celebration of these much maligned creatures. A search for other pigeon-related literature reveals a surprisingly varied array of books, scientific papers and websites dedicated to them, from both pigeon lovers (as distinct from 'fanciers') as well as those who wish to discourage and dispatch them. And much there is to know.

Doubtless, their close relationship with humans has made them easier objects for study than many other birds. It is a relationship that goes back a considerable way, certainly a thousand years and very likely a great deal more. Our connection with the ancestral Rock Dove extends even further back than that, although it is suggested (Johnston and Janiga, 1995) that by jointly considering the morphological, ecological and behavioural evidence available it is very probable that the Feral Pigeon, rather than in fact descending from just the Rock Dove, has originated from the lineages of at least eight different species of wild bird. It is, however, true to say that the Rock Dove was prominent in the early domestication of pigeons (Johnston and Janiga, 1995):

> "*Of the species of pigeons and doves still occurring in the Near East* [where early domestication would have taken place], *the rock pigeon had*

> *the right distributional, behavioural and reproductive characteristics to have been treated symbolically by Near Eastern people."*

The colonial nesting habits and presumed willingness to make 'voluntary' use of the early cityscapes as an alternative to their more 'natural' cliff and coastal nesting habitats would have made the Rock Dove an ideal candidate for initial capture and later domestication.

The birds and the people go back a very long way. Pigeon symbolism has been found that extends far back into the history of human civilisation. It is present in 6,500-year-old Mesopotamian artefacts and it is possible that humans were domesticating pigeons some 3,000 years ago. Whether 1,000 or 5,000 years ago (as per the lower and upper estimates), it is regarded as the earliest known domestication of any species of bird (Johnston and Janiga, 1995).

The pigeon has continued to play a part in human life throughout history, thanks to a great extent to their remarkable homing instincts that can see them safely home across hundreds of kilometres of unfamiliar country. It is a trait which is somewhat surprising, given the non-migratory, sedentary habits of the wild Rock Doves and their feral descendants. They were used by the Romans for message delivering, and a large network of pigeon-based communication was in place in parts of the Middle East 2,000 years BP (before present). Their more recent role during the First World War is better known when the birds were used for message carrying following military intelligence gathering from behind enemy lines. According to the Ministry of Defence, up to 20,000 pigeons were in use at various times throughout the war. Swift flying and adept as they proved to be at avoiding enemy rifles, they were an incredibly successful means of communication, with an impressive 95 per cent of birds finding their way through to their intended destinations and delivering often crucial information. Pigeons helped save the lives of many thousands during the slaughter of the Great War.

The homing instinct of the pigeon is indeed a fascinating thing as well as something of an enigma, with elements of it continuing to confound those dedicated to its study and evading conclusive definition. Theories are various, and each is apparently well supported by the evidence and observations of a great deal of scientific investigation. The so-called 'map and compass model' of pigeon navigation has long been thought to hold the secrets of their homing ability. The 'compass' part of the model means that the bird is able to orientate itself to a point on a compass without the use of familiar landmarks. It has been much suggested that orientation is achieved by the pigeons being able to judge the position of the sun at a given time of day. As the sun is not always visible, another method would be necessary and it seems that this is down to their ability to also employ a magnetic compass whereby special organs within the head allow them to sense, as many birds do, the Earth's magnetic field and to use that to determine their bearing.

The 'map' part requires the pigeon to be able to generate some kind of map with which to interpret any other directional information. It is this that provides the main source of mystery. They may follow visual landmarks when over familiar territory, while over unfamiliar terrain the sun and magnetism may well again be utilised but, such are the distances they can cover, this suggests that they employ an additional sense. Remarkably, it may be the case that pigeons can also navigate using their sense of smell. This is something that seems to have long been a source of intrigue. In 1922, when comparing the sense of smell of birds to that in other animals, W. H. Hudson (1841-1922) wrote (in *A Hind in Richmond Park*):

> *"Marvellous as is the sight in birds as compared with that of other animals, it appears probable that in some genera the sense of smell has not decayed as in the majority. I have never been able to find out the truth about the old notion regarding the pigeon's love of fragrant smells. This belief has actually led to actions at law brought by a man against his neighbour for having robbed him of his pigeons by attracting them to a new dovecot by that means. It is a question which might be settled by experiment."*

Indeed it might. Some fascinating experiments have been carried out to this end. One such investigation (Gagliardo *et al.*, 1999) involved 'doctoring' two groups of 24 birds. One group had the trigeminal nerve disabled, the pigeon's so-called magnetoreceptors located at the base of the bill. The other pigeons where denied the use of their olfactory nerves in a similar way. On releasing each group of pigeons 50 kilometres from their loft – one to the south, the other to the north – all but one of those that maintained their sense of smell and not their magnetic sense returned home within 24 hours of being released. Only four of those without the ability to smell made it back to the loft and took longer than the other birds in doing so.

It may be that a pigeon will learn much of the information it requires to perform this feat in the early months of its life. Another experiment involved three groups of pigeons reared through the first three or four months of their 'post-fledgling' lives, each under different conditions. One group was kept in an aviary screened from any scent-bearing winds. As 'controls', one group was held in an aviary but given exposure to the wind and the other allowed to fly freely. At about six months past the age of fledging they were released from distant release sites. The 'free-flying' and 'unscreened' birds had no difficulty in guiding themselves back, whereas those deprived the benefits of the information blown in on the winds *"were unable to orientate homeward and...were generally unsuccessful in returning home"* (Gagliardo *et al.*, 2001).

Both experiments may well have resulted in a handful of somewhat confused, rather lost, but presumably still healthy pigeons, but what intriguing possibilities have they helped to reveal about that intangibilities of the natural world? Most recently it has even been suggested that pigeons are using ultra-low frequency sound waves to construct a kind of acoustic map to help them get around — the plot thickens further. Regardless of theories, we give little credit to how much experience of our environment exists beyond the limitation of our senses. The image of the Feral Pigeons on the high street too stupid to get out from under our feet or away from the wheels of our cars as we virtually stop to let them flutter out of danger is fading by the minute.

Quite unaware of the astonishing things that go on inside a pigeon's brain, I nonetheless continued with much interest to watch my car park birds for some minutes further, finding myself a great deal more engaged than I normally would be in their behaviour. I gradually became aware of a growing significance of the situation in my mind. A handful of cars had been arriving with kick-off approaching and others carrying those buying tickets for the forthcoming first-team matches arriving and departing the club shop. The outdoor market that has been held in the car park for years was being packed up and so there were those vehicles also making their way out. And amid these comings and goings in an out-of-the-way, dusty corner of the car park a little drama was being enacted.

It was almost like my own modern-day and rather more light-hearted version of what Richard Jefferies had observed more than a century before, of those pigeons (*The Life of Fields*) that had taken up residence on the walls of a museum. Within them he imbued the sense of freedom that can be missing in the town and city, with the concerns that modern living can place upon us. That the *"mental toil"* in the library of the great building and the *"lading of the waggons in the street"* is an irrelevance to them and that theirs is *"the air and light"*, just as it had been when the birds inhabited the temples in which the statues within the museum once stood so many centuries before. Here is a metaphor, albeit unlikely in the minds of most to include the Feral Pigeon, that rings so true in our own time, perhaps even more so. Very probably I was the only person that had had the inclination to notice the birds in Southend that afternoon; had taken the time to watch and similarly allowed my thoughts, momentarily, to be transported far away from the circumstances of my location.

Through the activities of the aforementioned two — briefly three — pigeons engrossed in courtship the real wildness of nature was being expressed, irrespective of how contrived the scene and the subjects may supposedly have been. Just the same as if it were Great Crested Grebe performing their wonderful display of 'penguin dancing' on the silent waters of some tranquil lake, or male and female Marsh Harrier swooping over a reed-covered fenland expanse, passing prey to each other while in flight and tumbling in the air. Even though the actions of these are, on the face of it, very different and often more obviously wondrous or spectacular, the essence of each of the three behaviours is identical. The fact that two of these happen to involve the full majesty of large birds of prey on the wing or the elegant movements of beautiful water birds and the other the overly familiar and bothersome presence of the town pigeon is in this context quite irrelevant. The prerogatives are as important, the drives behind them equally as strong. So too are the challenges they face. The acquisition of food for the Feral Pigeon may well be closely aligned with human activities, either through our willingness to feed them or our general untidiness, but in every other respect they must carry out their life cycles in the face of all the pressures of living in the wild: "*If their offspring survive, they will have done so despite considerable environmental resistance.*"

Often, since my 'pigeon epiphany' in the car park, I have noticed them more frequently or observed them more closely. I have found myself looking out for them at times when they have not been immediately obvious. I have tried to count them near where I live; maybe as many as 200 huddled on the roofs of the shops along the main road. And on one occasion, waiting for a train at Paddington, I even allowed myself to do something I very likely had not done since I was a lad on a school trip to Trafalgar Square – I fed them! A man beside me was enjoying a pasty but was evidently uncomfortable with the inevitable pigeon pecking up the crumbs around his feet, lifting up a foot and feigning a kick toward the persistent and hungry bird. I felt moved to pinch off a corner of the sandwich in my packed lunch to sprinkle on the ground as a small and silent protest on behalf of pigeon-kind.

If ever we needed a lesson that the things of nature are so rarely as they seem at first glance, it is surely from the pigeon that we can learn as much as any. They might also remind us of how we can take the obvious so very much for granted. I am sure on this last point that, with the pigeon in mind, there will be some readers who will take more convincing than is offered here, but as far as our engagement with its living components is concerned, our world has become all too contrived. Our focus seems increasingly diverted away from such things and towards the altogether more trivial, towards control and deterrent rather than simple and usually quite effortless coexistence and small compromises.

By coincidence, while I was actually collecting these pigeon-related thoughts, a cold-caller canvassing for work knocked at my door to offer me his services of, among other things, the removal of lichen and moss from the roof tiles. I explained that we weren't especially worried about the moss on the roof to which he seemed mildly surprised, and that was pretty much that. And why should I be? They — the mosses and lichens — don't seem to be causing any serious problems, although I suppose in theory a piece of lichen if given long enough could work its way into the tiles, but how long would they need? Not that I get to look at them very often, but I do quite like the idea of them being there and who knows what lichen-feeding invertebrate is eking out an existence above our heads. More than one species of moss- and lichen-feeding moth has been lured in by the bathroom light in the past and, besides, there are numerous other things I would need to attend to before worrying about what some passer-by might think of my roof.

I do appreciate, of course, that it is rather easier for me to fight the corner of the pigeon as I don't have to contend with the extent of guano-related mess that others have to deal with. We do, though, have the good old town foxes to contend with, what with their liking for earthworms (irrespective of what plants they need to dig up in order to get to them), our rubbish bins and, not least, their astonishingly prolific digestive systems and predilection for emptying it in the most inopportune of locations. I would, however, much rather spend time innovating simple ways through which to minimise their disruption whilst still enjoying their presence in the neighbourhood rather than attempt to deter them altogether. Some of our neighbours I suspect would not entirely agree. But like the fox and the lichen in each of their own ways, the Feral Pigeon is actually, when all is considered, quite a remarkable creature.

But why devote a chapter, one might reasonably ask having just read it, in a book not necessarily about pigeons, to the pigeon. I would hope that these commonplace birds demonstrate all those things mentioned at the outset; how nature resides in unlikely quarters, even amid the austerity of the city, and how it is so very easily overlooked. They might also present us with a microcosm of a wider view of nature that is not restricted to wild places but which infiltrates even the most urban of landscapes. We watch the wildlife documentaries and marvel at the extravagances of the weird and wonderful that grace our TV screens but far less likely direct a moment's thought for the admittedly less exotic, but no less tenacious, remarkably adaptive and highly evolved creatures that live all around us. It is within such things that we might first realise a connection with the natural world that we have long thought missing from our lives. Heavy praise for the tiresome pigeon? Well, it's not as if I'm the first to have been moved to write about them.

The Lay of the Land

> *"Many historians stick to documents and are reluctant to put on their boots and ask questions of the land and the things that grow on it."*
>
> Oliver Rackham (*The Illustrated History of the Countryside*)

From the places that help comprise the day-to-day of our lives and the living things that reside within them, to the very land in which they exist. To our own history and beyond – that of place, of country and continents. The faintly coalescing histories of the millennia that have passed before with relative empirical silence. Each has draped their layers of substance over the bare bones of the land. In remembering how to look, we may also have to listen. The land speaks to us; it's just a question of being able to understand what it's saying.

The geologists listen. They listen to the most ancient voices of the land. Voices that recall the ages of tremendous violence and unspeakable turmoil. Of raging fires and boiling rocks. Voices of unimaginable patience and of taking the strain. Of the land frozen, gouged, torn and heaved. Voices that are stubborn, but ultimately relenting. Voices that tell some of the most graphic of tales.

The words in places may be lost, muffled by the strata and immensity of Earth history. In others it manages to find a way to be heard – sometimes quite loudly. With such localities in mind, where better than the Lake District to 'listen' and see the passage of geological time laid out before us. As Douglas Botting confirms in *Wild Britain*: "*In few other parts of England are visitors more immediately aware of the land than in the Lake District.*" A hike up to the top of Hay Stacks, perhaps. A fell of modest proportions, not quite 600 metres above sea level, with a summit that reaches about half a kilometre above the shore of

Buttermere below. Of modest proportions maybe, but whose craggy buttresses towering up ahead are instantly striking to those that approach them. Such scenery, as to be seen over much of the central Lake District, is hewn from volcanic rocks, the product of a great cataclysm that occurred about 450 million years ago and which heaved up through the layers of sediment-derived slates of similar age. The legacy is the rugged splendour and antiquity beyond simple comprehension. Where the violence that wrought them still echoes in the roughness of the landscape, the challenging accents and the near-on sheer ridges that demand our respect.

From the surroundings of the adjacent lakes of Buttermere and Crummock Water, the land sweeps upwards, moderately at first and then more abruptly. With Hay Stacks rising up on one side, the steep slopes beneath Fleetwith Pike to the other and a curving collar of crags connecting the two, the effect is to create a towering amphitheatre of stone. With its walls ascending, the reverse view is no less revealing of the landscape. From below the summit of Hay Stack, the ground drops alarmingly away. Looking back – across the amphitheatre approach, past the two lakes, almost abutting each other end to end, each reflecting the angle of the other and on through distant fells – you might almost think that you can gain an inkling of the vast channel of ice, hundreds of metres thick, that carved its way through and over ground many thousands of years previously.

Across to the other side of the broad ridge of Hay Stacks, the valley of Ennerdale down below narrows along the course of the River Liza, out of its conifer-shadowed environs and at its apex rising steeply (300 metres higher up than Hay Stacks) to the hulking, decidedly handsome figure of Great Gable, one of the Lake District's loftier peaks. The long Lakeland history is again spread out before us. The volcanic origins of the great domed summit, the ice and water-weathered valley stretched out beneath. Each silvery strand of the distant becks, as they tumble down from the high slopes, are accompanied by the darker shadows of their unwavering carving of the rocks about them, even through the millennia of calmer times remaining so patient and relentless and another echo of the greater forces that shaped this land.

It is so often our mountains, here and elsewhere, that have the most to say of our land's most ancient origins – its bones indeed laid bare. Our wildest country unfolds across the Highlands of Scotland, rolling on for mile after mile across the Grampians and over the Northwest Highlands, encompassing all of the lonely magnificence of such a mountainous expanse – the stunning drama of the sweeping glens and brooding tranquillity of the lochs that striate and punctuate the landscape in their hundreds, even thousands.

With its old fault lines, most famously the Great Glen fault, and 400-million-year-old mountains thrust up from the Earth's crust, it reminds for us a time when Britain would have sat on the edge of a continental plate boundary. And it is a landscape that may tell of ages much, much further back. In the far north-west there are rocks that tell the oldest tales of any place in the British Isles; they are among the oldest in the world. Here there are to be found rocks known as gneiss (pronounced 'nice'). They recall an age when unimaginable heat, huge pressures and a great deal of time metamorphosised the shales and mudstones – made from fine particles deposited by the waters of an ancient sea – into slates and schists, and eventually into gneisses. It is an age that murmurs through the interpretation of the most fundamental structures of the rocks: the proportional presence of isotopes, the atomic variations of chemical elements, like uranium or lead, with a known rate of decay and that can persist over millions upon millions of years. The north-west Scottish gneisses date back more than 2,700 million years. These might be among the quietest voices of the land, which only a few may be able to interpret, but voices still calling nevertheless across the numberless centuries.

Even in those places without the drama of aeons passed etched into the shapes and surfaces of its timeless vistas, the ageless voices of the land and its origins can still be heard. It might reverberate more softly across the gently rolling hills than the giddying sight of soaring mountains. It will often be less assertive among the quiet intensity of the lowland wood than the birches and mountain ash that cling to the sides of the plunging, water-worn upland valleys. The empty, sky-filled panorama of the gaping estuary that extrapolates the flatness of the abutting lands far out into and away to the endless horizon can only accommodate a whisper compared to the cacophony of foaming breakers, snarling rocks and the booming, towering cliff face. Softer, less assertive and quieter it may be, but still it is a voice forceful enough to persist, like the others, throughout the countless passing years. It is a voice that the botanist would certainly hear and so too, perhaps, the naturalist of wider interest. It is one that transcends the ancient words of rock and stone (although never forgetting its origins) into a more contemporary language of real-time life-cycles, of growth and seasons. It is the language of leaf and seed, flowers and even pollen.

The plants that grow in a place can inform us of a great deal beyond merely their presence before our eyes. They may do much to translate the archaic words into those of the here and now, into the attention of the generations that pass beneath their boughs and through their swathes – or at least of those that remain! A far cry from the Lakeland Fells it may be, but it is to my home county of Essex that I am inclined to refer to illustrate my point.

The rocks that underlie modern-day Essex have long been buried by the various clays, sands and alluvia set down by millions of years of rising and falling prehistoric seas, long diverted rivers and the scouring of ice-age glaciers and the outwashing of their meltwaters. The rock underneath all of this is the chalk formed at the bottom of an ancient sea, more than

65 million years ago, from the accumulated remains of trillions of prehistoric, microscopic algae. Chalk surfaces in the county only at its southern and north-western extremities.

Even with much to interpret, to study the map of the county's surface geology reveals a clear north-west/south-east split. The erosive and depositing activities of the river courses in the area aside, the great majority of the north-western half of the map is coloured by the British Geological Survey quite obviously and strikingly different to the opposite half. The pattern of glaciation during the millions of years of ice ages, up until as recently as 12,000 years ago, explains why. On its passage across the land to the north, ice gouged huge quantities of so-called Chalky Boulder Clay. The advancing ice sheets never made it as far as the south-east of Essex, due in part to a ridge of relatively high land running diagonally across the central part of the county, thus burying the land to the north-west with their collected substrate whilst leaving the area to the south-east uncovered.

It is through the plants and their sensitivity to the soil around their roots that allows the chill roar of the Arctic ice that once dominated these lands so many years ago, to whisper on the warming breeze of spring and through the hazy heat of summer. Certain calcicole (chalk-loving) plants can only find their optimal conditions among the chalk-rich Boulder Clay. Some others with no tolerance for alkaline soils (calcifuge plants) must grow elsewhere to thrive. Thus our flora might trace this very basic arrangement of the geology of the soil.

Stanley T. Jermyn (1909-73) provides the maps and a historical perspective in his posthumously published *Flora of Essex* (1974) (sadly many of the current plant distributions detailed in this book have retracted drastically since). Many plant species are quite unfussy as to what constitutes appropriate growing conditions. Not so however, the Clustered Bellflower, Greater Burnet-saxifrage, Yellow-wort and Wayfaring tree, scattered predominantly across the north-western quarter of the county. Nor the Ling or Hard Fern exhibiting a distinct southern and easterly distribution. Taking this a step further, the distribution of certain plants will have obvious implications for the occurrence of certain animals, invertebrates in particular. The Gorse Shield Bug, for example, is yet to be recorded in the north-western quarter of the county where its food plant is much scarcer (Gorse favours light, sandy soils – conditions not especially prevalent on areas of heavy clay), a pattern by and large followed by such moths as the Narrow-winged Pug, Autumnal Rustic and Fox Moth, all associated with heather and heathland and generally unknown outside the southern and eastern reaches. To superimpose, in the mind's eye, the distribution maps of such species over the geological map of Essex conjures a wonderfully simple illustration of the past and present combined and of the land very much communicating to us more of the secrets of its history. Doubtless, a mixed expertise in botany, geology and many other disciplines besides would make for a progressively and satisfyingly more complex image; the consequences of sandy soil and salt spray from the coast, or the vagaries of soil moisture and aspect to the sunlight for instance. Such things, after all, are the reasons for nature's variety, its subtleties of adaptation and exploitation, a match for its vast diversity and indeed our boundless fascination with it. Even in its simpler terms, however, such connections demonstrate the relationship of plant and soil, living and the non-living, that spans the millennia back into the dimmest and most distant past.

It is not only the living plants that echo the stories of the pre-historic landscape. Maybe not strictly speaking falling within the remit of the modern, living landscape giving up the secrets of the aeons, but plants many centuries dead may still have the ability to speak to us by means of pollen grains shed onto the ground and scattered across forgotten landscapes. These may be preserved, particularly in layers of peat or lake sediment that built up over time. Even though, as Oliver Rackham points out in his book *The Illustrated History of the Countryside*, pollen analysis does have its limitations (not all plants produce pollen grains that are as easily seen as others under a microscope and neither will they necessarily produce them in comparable quantities), a core of such substrate, once extracted and investigated, can offer a wealth of information on the vegetation of the past. As Rackham also reminds us, it is the evidence of pollen analysis that tells us what we know of the tree communities of the wildwood, the ancestral woodland that came to cover the greater part of Britain following the last Ice Age some 12,000 years ago and from which our modern woodland is descended.

So indeed, prehistoric pollen tells a tale or two and not only about the wild places but also about the movements of our own ancestors within them. For instance, and once again using Essex as an example, Peter Murphy (1996), writing on the *Environmental Archaeology of Essex*, refers to a period in the pollen record for the south-west of the county that indicates a decline in elm and an increase in cereal and Ribwort Plantain pollen (the last being regarded as something of an arable weed). This apparently shows that by 2,600 BP the Essex farmer had well and truly honed his agricultural skills long before that time and had already achieved a significant clearing of the wildwood for his crops.

Staying among the woods and returning to the living plants of today, it is they that may still tell of antiquity, perhaps not as far back as the wildwood proper but providing a murmur nevertheless uttered over many centuries. For the ecologist and historian, a wood is either ancient or secondary. Officially, the area of the former must have been continuously wooded since at least the 17th century. Many woods may be traced back much further still. The age of wood might be determined by researching old maps or even older, historical surveys, such as the Doomsday Book of the 11th century.

With an ecologist's eye, a wood's age may also be suggested by the plants growing within it, the so-called 'ancient woodland indicator species'. Some woodland plants are known to occur (introductions not withstanding) more usually or even exclusively in very old woodland. According to lists of indicator species gathered by Keith Kirby for Natural England (Rose, 2006), a wood containing the likes of Sweet Woodruff, Wood Anemone and Yellow Archangel, along with Wood Melick, Great and Hairy Woodrush and Wood Sedge, is very likely to be of ancient origin. Not only herbaceous and grassy plants, but trees and shrubs also will give strong clues to the age of a wood, such as the Midland Hawthorn and Wild Service (see Rackham in Rose, 2006). Once again, we might look at the flora of a place as a thing of beauty, texture and sensory stimulation, but also as store of information accessible to those with the eyes and ears for it.

From the past, more distant than most of us can properly comprehend and through the still so very murky mists of time, the land will indeed answer many of the questions asked of it. Taking a more contemporary view (in relative Earth history terms at any rate), we humans have made a habit of inadvertently adding our clues to the answers of the questions we might, at some point, ask. The land has its topography: the shapes dictated fundamentally by the unceasing forces deep within the Earth and the sculpting hand of those most elemental forces of nature: wind, water and ice. Yet to this we might still add our mark and, with our human nature, that which we cannot change we will look to record nevertheless. We have added our own more finely detailed sculptured topographies to the geological heave and swell.

Our countryside is scattered with the artefacts of human life over the centuries that tell of agriculture, ownership or even politics. Voices that are unobtrusively persistent even through the days of bulldozers and JCBs. Ancient woodlands are rarely without their woodbanks. Larger woods might be divided up by them, as imprints of the former rights of commoners to their produce and use for their livestock. Some may be relatively recent, many can be dated to the Middle Ages and some further back to Saxon days. A bank along the edge of a wood could mark the line of a parish boundary. Indeed, this might also be the case with interior woodbanks. There is a wood in south Essex, which is presumably one of many more in other parts of the country that is traversed by such a bank, with one half of the wood residing in the parish of Hadleigh, the other in Thundersley. Not quite the 'three-counties view' that greets those afloat along the bends of the River Wye, beneath Symonds Yat, where the boundaries of Herefordshire, Worcestershire and Monmouthshire meet, but a point of interest nonetheless, and no doubt one of many small secrets that may be conveyed by some map or other.

In places, the land of the open countryside still bears the undulations of old farming systems. As Rackham explains, the 'open-field' of medieval times was apportioned into 'sellions', strips of land measuring one furlong by two perches – 220 by 11 yards (about 200 by 10 metres). The owners of each strip cultivated the ground themselves. The ploughing of these narrow strips tended to heap the soil towards the middle of the plot, resulting in the so-called 'ridge and furrow' that in many parts of England and Scotland still ripples the surface of the land today. More distant messages come from the likes of the earthworks and hut circles of the Bronze Age reaves that cover parts of Dartmoor, carrying meaning that has filtered through from perhaps as long as 3,000 years ago, maybe more. And if one was to look on many an Ordnance Survey Explorer map, there will likely be a scattering of tumuli or barrows, the mounds built over the burial chambers of the late Neolithic and Bronze Age dead.

Therefore, the cartographer (with a certain amount of help from the archaeologist) also listens to the voices of the land and often with very great attention to detail. Such voices, of course, might be our own, amplified to be audible across the generations. It is here that I must confess something of a small obsession…maps. Google Earth is, I would be quick to admit, amazing, and the potential of having electronic maps loaded onto a small portable screen is undeniably great. But they cannot be a true match for a proper paper map. When planning a journey or devising walking routes, with sheets of Ordnance Survey Explorer maps spread out across the floor, their tactile element is a very important thing. A two-dimensional representation of a three-dimensional landscape it may be, but there is a kind of depth to them that a computer screen cannot deliver, mainly because the latter do not offer the benefit of many square kilometres available for simultaneous perusal. Just as the internet has yet to sound the death knell for the book, so too will the map hopefully enjoy similar immunity.

For me perusing Ordnance Survey (OS) maps is an essential part of any holiday and exploration of new places. There is no replacement for actually getting out there yourself, but there is a pleasure to be taken from first studying a map. Following the course of streams into rivers. Tracing the contours meandering across the paper. Noting how the woods, lakes, wetlands or even the settlements fit into the scene. All the time trying to imagine the landscape from the cues and clues on the map. Placing yourself on some craggy ridge and visualising the plunge of the mountainside, told to you by the darkening orange of retracting contour lines. Or perhaps sat among the quietly teeming fenland, the fringing expanse of wind-rippled reeds opening up on a sweeping bend of a river, curving away before a sun-hazed, cattle-grazed marsh and the tranquillity beyond, all things made evident by the similarly sinuous, but more spacious contours of flowing curves and broad expanses.

It turns out that this is an obsession, one I have rarely felt inclined to admit to, shared with others, not least Alfred

Wainwright (1907-1991), who once wrote in *A Pennine Journey*:

> *"Give me a map of country I know, and I am comforted...Give me the map of country I do not know, even of country I shall never know, and it has the power to thrill and excite me."*

He too relished the anticipation of visiting a new place, an anticipation built through the studious pouring over the map beforehand. Also in the prompting of memories of past expeditions, of the layering of those memories upon the lines of the map. Maps are souvenirs of holidays and experiences, lasting reminders that are so much more meaningful than the great majority of artefacts that fills the shelves of tourist shops and visitor centres the country over. For Wainwright a map was a most personal belonging. They were *"old friends, understood only by the man with whom they have travelled the miles."* A map to the traveller is layered with experience, emotion and nostalgia. Each map is in this way unique. Its 'identical-ness' to any other copy of the same is restricted to the representation of the country printed onto its surface. Subjectively though, each is so very much more than mere paper and ink. Two people could walk the same route with the same map but, as means of recollection and storytelling, it could never be the same to each.

Maps can offer the means to explore with confidence off the more regularly beaten track. They indeed might take you across some of those less-peopled Lakeland Fells. Up the less-popular but still spectacular Snowdonian peaks and a heightened sense of solitude. And to less well-known beaches hidden away among the rocky shores of the stunning Cornish coastline.

It is something of a triumph that the two-dimensional rendering of the rise and fall, or even just the gentle relief of the rolling landscape, can be presented in such a way as to create in the imagination a world of depth and eventfulness, and so accurately too. With a little experience of the maps and interpreting them on the ground, the two almost become one. This is something that can clearly prove most useful.

Walking in the Berwyn Mountains of Wales in August is a very fine thing to do. My companion Lola and I made an early start at the magnificent Pistyll Rhaedr, Wales' highest waterfall at 80 metres, to ensure that the inevitable crowds were avoided, providing an even more delightful start to our hike up to the summit of Moel Sych. The outward route traversed one flank of a small, fairly steep-sided, bracken-clothed valley, before angling across a relatively flat stretch of heather-tinged ground to the foot of the short and reasonably sharp ascent up to the summit. Moel Sych, at 827 metres above sea level, occupies one of several crag-topped arcs along a ridge of higher ground. Immediately south is a lesser, unnamed conglomeration of stone, some 130 metres lower, and to the north Cadair Berwyn, at the same height as Moel Sych, and further on Cadair Bronwen 50 metres lower. Together they comprise a short chain, about five kilometres in length. A satisfyingly rugged and prominent destination for the walker and something effectively and enticingly represented on the OS map.

The return route was a more gradual and less eventful descent southwards back towards the waterfall. At least that is what we intended. During a brief moment of complacency and the elation of being among such wonderful surroundings – the spread of mountain and moorland on all sides, our lofty viewpoint from which we could trace our route upwards, the entertainment of a group of Raven tumbling and frolicking on some rising column of warm air – we set off along the wrong track. As we negotiated our way across our sodden, moss-cushioned path we did raise an eyebrow or two at the state of what we were still assuming to be a fairly well-used route. As we walked on (or should that be paddled on?), the expected steep drop to the left didn't arrive, the land sloping away on both sides with far less urgency than it should have. The warning lights flashed on. Another look at the map confirmed our error. The longer we had continued along our course, the magnitude of our 'faux pas' would have increased disproportionately to the distance travelled. As it was, a quick bit of corner cutting added no more than a kilometre onto our journey and we soon rejoined the correct path, acting quite, as far as our fellow walkers would have discerned, as if nothing had gone awry. The land, along with the map, had spoken and eventually we had listened. No wonder Wainwright dedicated the first of his Lakeland guidebooks to 'The Men of the Ordnance Survey'.

Maps are all about translating the language of the landscape, of its expanse, its shapes, its profiles and textures, into one more easily and more comprehensively understood. Also, as briefly mentioned earlier, they also say a lot about the human requirement for recording things. We might unfold our map and, with a need to plot a route or plan a journey, concentrate on the roads and footpaths and perhaps also the rise and fall of the ground, or the position of larger features, such as woods, rivers and lakes. But there really is an incredible quantity of information contained on them. Nearly everything has a name. The tiny copse of trees. The branching tributaries of winding streams contributing to the catchments of greater rivers. The hills, commons, lanes and bridges. The bogs and marshes. And, of course, the names of places, of settlements. To make mention of all this feels rather like stating the obvious, but a good map is a very remarkable thing.

Even at face value, the breadth of information on offer is substantial, but so often these names will tell us more about the areas that they mark out. To explore the origins of place names is a whole different ball game itself and would reveal stories enough to fill their own books, as indeed they have.

Many of these stories will already be blurred by the passage of time, but there may be someone somewhere with a nugget of information that sheds light and shows the way to further discovery. But even a rudimentary consideration of the names of just our towns and villages, rivers and hills adds a little depth to the breadth of detail contained on the map. In this, the words of Alan Brownjohn in his poem *For a Journey* (in Brownjohn *et al.*, 1969) have some resonance:

> *"Who knows what could become of you where*
> *No one has understood the place with names?"*

This whole idea of place names had largely existed outside of my sphere of interest and was something I had given little thought to. However, a ten pence investment from a book stall at a local fête encouraged a small and satisfying shift in this general direction. The book in question was no less than *The Shell Country Book*, written by Geoffry Grigson (1905-85) and published in 1962. Grigson was a writer, poet and critic of some note before his death in 1985. It seems he achieved as much notoriety as he did accolades for his work, of which there was a great deal. As a writer he was the author of many essays and much poetry, and as a critic he was unflinching and made his fair share of enemies among literary circles.

Grigson also had a great interest, as I would discover from the bargain I had bagged for myself (ten pence well spent I'd say), in the countryside and its flora, fauna and traditions. The book included several chapters devoted to the names of places, rivers and hills. He begins the chapter entitled *Names of Places* by telling us: *"Names of places are odd things, not to be trifled with, and often meaning something they do not appear to mean."* Having found a little bit out about the man, do we hear just a hint of his supposedly stern character? We are left in no doubt as to the seriousness of the matter at hand. These are cautionary words echoed elsewhere. A. D. Mills in his *Dictionary of English*

Place Names advises us that the *"instant etymologies"* of even the most apparently obvious meanings are *"usually a delusion"*. Such misguided assumption is well illustrated by the villages of Upper and Lower Slaughter in Gloucester, named not for the obvious reference to the dispatching of livestock but very likely from the Old English 'slohtre' – a 'muddy place'. Language is more fluid than we normally realise, given the limited experience of our own lifetimes. With subtle but persistent change over the centuries, the names of places, perhaps 1,000 years old or more, may have been tweaked or corrupted, sometimes by condensation, their true meaning becoming lost over time beneath the layers of linguistic evolution. Nevertheless, even Grigson concedes, that when out and about *"one can keep in mind (with caution) a few possibilities"*.

The familiar components of our city, town and village names reveal something of the former appearance of our landscapes. A place ending in -wich, for example, will often refer historically to a dairy farm and the suffix -ham would likely have denoted a meadow surrounded by water or marshland, or perhaps a village or homestead. In the southwest, -combe means valley, taken from the Welsh word cwm, while names incorporating -chester, -caster or -cester would have been given to settlements with fortifications or earthworks, derived from the Latin castre and the Old English ceaster, meaning fort of encampment. And remembering the warning against taking some place names at face value, the -ton at the end of a name is unlikely to refer to a 'town', but rather a farm or manor, and a place suffixed with -port will not necessarily refer to a seaport, even if the place happens to be by the sea; rather it meant, according to Grigson, *"a town with the right to hold a market (a town with walls and a town gate, porta in Latin)."*

Not in relation to our towns but also the labelling of the physical aspects of our landscapes can add extra depth and understanding to the imagination and the two dimensions on the map. Consider some of the names that we have given to ranges of hills. The Malverns in Worcestershire, for instance, have a name that means 'bare hill', a development of the Welsh words moel bryn. The name Mendip, for that most pleasant range of Somerset hills, is likely to mean little more than 'mountain' (or perhaps more accurately, in terms of its stature, 'hill'), from the Welsh 'mynydd' or the Celtic 'mönïth'. Although not really of mountainous proportions, these hills do rise in striking fashion from the relatively flat lands that spread away at their feet. The names of rivers, too, might give us a sense of the landscape before we actually visit it. The Lynn that careers down the steep cleft in the land at Lynton and Lynmouth in Exmoor is so named for the speed at which it flows, from the Old English hllynn, meaning a torrent. A river's environs rather than its movement may be reflected in the name. The Cornish River Fowey means the 'the river of the beech trees'.

The name of the River Dart that thunders and foams its way through Dartmoor also originates from the nature of the woods at its banks, with 'dart' being the old Devonian word for oak. Anyone who has explored the glorious Dart Valley knows that the place is almost as much about its enveloping oak woods that fill the narrow plain of the river and cling to the steep valley slopes as it is about the river itself that crashes its way around long tumbled granite boulders, with its ever-shifting waters, crystal clear and restful during its calmer stretches and then entrancing, white water torrent the next. It is fitting that such a fine river should be accompanied on its course by old woods of equal beauty and that the woods should be cleaved in such wonderfully dramatic fashion. Where the cut and thrust of the Gold-ringed Dragonfly is so easily exchanged for the elegant beauty of the Silver-washed Fritillary, and the diminutive poise of the Pied Flycatcher, aptly replaced so naturally by the derring-do of the torrent-hopping

Dipper.

Such examples as the few cited above really represent the more obvious features of the names on our maps; the location of voices that are more easily detected should we want to listen to them. But what other whispers inhabit the human landscape and the world set down onto paper? The lesser voices of people long gone from the countryside, but still there to be heard. Who was the man called 'Haukr', in possession of the Cumbrian mountain pasture, 800 years ago, after which the village of Hawkshead was named? And what of 'Seawulf', or 'Sigewulf', whose farmstead in Saxon Northamptonshire most likely became the Silverstone of our modern day? Normal folk among the communities of their times perhaps, but with voices that for some reason have been sustained over time. Maybe their personal dramas and every-day tribulations did encompass stories of significance and interest. Either scenario in its own right would be intriguing enough to us of the modern day. The maps and landscapes alike still speak quietly, not just of towns, villages, waterways and rolling hills but also of lineages and human endeavour. Of work and of actions, process and progress. Within this lies something of the nature's *"enormous value"* in respect *"of its role as a cultural archive, a record of human endeavour and husbandry"* spoken of by the conservationist W.M. (Bill) Adams.

And not only is it our ancestors that leave the traces of their passing for the browser of the map. The knowledge of wild creatures and plants are scattered throughout, within the names of our settlements. Fleeting though it is, do we capture a snapshot of the wildlife watchers of old? Perhaps, but the motives for their observations would surely have often been very much borne from utilitarian needs, rather than purely botanical or otherwise. The old names for trees were often called upon. The timber and other resources to be obtained from lind (lime), withig (willow) and hessle (hazel) would naturally, one assumes, become focal points for local communities for reasons other than aesthetics, as they may have been at Lindridge (Worcestershire), Withycombe (Somerset) and Hesleden (County Durham). The derivations of such place names are reasonably obvious, with the knowledge, at least, of the archaic names of the plants and animals from which they were gleaned. In other instances this is clearer still. Otterbourne in Hampshire refers to a stream frequented by Otters, and Ottershaw, a small Surrey wood. Ravenscar in North Yorkshire was named after a rock much visited by Ravens, and Birchover in Derbyshire from 'a ridge where birches grow'. It would be wise here to note, however, that neither Otterington (North Yorkshire) and Otteringham (Humberside) were named after Otters but a man called 'Oter', and the Essex village name of Birch comes not from the tree but the Old English *bryce*, meaning 'land recently broken up for cultivation'. Once again, we have been warned!

Many references to flora and fauna, needless to say, can be very obscure. Obscure and all the more intriguing for it. Why would the Oxfordshire pool at Finmere and the farmstead at Finstock have been particularly associated with woodpeckers? For whatever reason we are now able to assume that Snipe or Bittern would often be seen in the wood or clearing at Purleigh in Essex and at Purley in Berkshire. So too the sandpiper or Dunlin that would have been known to any Saxon birdwatchers in the Gloucestershire valley at Stinchcombe and the ford at Dorset's Stinsford. And what was it about the nook of land in the Cheshire countryside at Marthall and the Norfolk homestead at Martham that was so attractive to weasels or martens, enough to be named after them?

The landscape of Britain has changed much over the centuries since these names were first coined, in most places quite drastically so. As A.D. Mills aptly observes: "*The interest of a place-name does not stop at its meaning and derivation: rather these provide the basic and essential starting point for the fuller appreciation of a place-name's significance."* In many instances, no doubt, the features of the land – its habitats and habitation – would today bear little resemblance to clues offered by the names. The 'mossy spring' at Muswell Hill would take some finding, like so many of the various farmsteads, woodland clearings and heathland enclaves that contributed their presence to the name of so many of our settlements. But these names do offer us an albeit faint and fading impression of a time and times long before our own, which if we were of a mind to piece everything together would provide us with a reference point for how much our world has changed. Try to imagine a Britain where the Wild Cat (catt) stalked the East Anglian marshlands at Cattawade and the Wolf (ulfr) roamed the Cumbrian wilderness around Ulpha. These are evocative thoughts to the modern day naturalist.

The land clings tightly to its history, ensuring that even the faintest of messages persist, however weakly. Simply by being there, it still has a great deal to tell us, of its wildlife and its people. A good deal more too than that contained within the pages of this chapter. It has many voices with which to speak and not just for the benefit of the geologist, botanist or cartographer and historian, but for everyone. It is, as the quote heading this chapter suggests, just a question of asking it the right things. Each voice is different but rarely discrete from the others. The Earth, its plants (and with its plants we can make judgements also of its animal life) and people can never be viewed in isolation – it would seem foolhardy to attempt to do so. One influences the other and another in turn, and our perceptions of each shaping the way in which we listen and learn. And each voice may be interpreted differently, questioned to a different degree, to yield as much or as little of their secrets as we ask.

The Pool: a lesson in looking

Even by mid-morning the heat has filled the air. Around each straight trunk of the Calabrian Pine trees and across the needle-littered, kindling-dry forest floor. The sun already bouncing its blaze off the forest road, to the liking of the grasshoppers which are springing about with a flash of their predator-confusing red wings and disappearing in an instant among the stones. The pale limestone rocks are already something more than warm to the touch. The cicadas among the treetops, in full, shrill voice, serve only to intensify the growing heat of the day with an aural intensity.

The high summer in south-west Turkey can feel uncompromising. The afternoon heat may be intense, so much so that it can seem as if even some of the sun-lovers have had more than their fill or at least feel a need to take temporary leave from the soaring temperatures. Great Banded Grayling butterflies flit in and out of the shade of the shadowing trees to settle cryptically on tree trunks and rocks in the dappled sunlight. With broad white bands daubed parallel to the body, across the upperside of the wings that can span up to eight centimetres, this is one of the larger and, for the brief time their wings remain open, certainly one of the most striking of the 'browns'. The much smaller Large Wall Brown skim across the rides, setting down at the edge of the track, with their wings held teasingly open, before quickly flicking them shut; the beautiful eyed markings on the subtly marked, stony-grey underside of the hindwings are arguably their better side. The grasses on which both of these butterflies lay their eggs appear so parched and withered as to surely not provide sufficient nourishment to the caterpillars that feed on them. But provide they clearly do; neither species seems an uncommon sight along the forest roads.

A coincidence it may be that the butterflies tend to frequent the semi-shade, but for other cold-blooded creatures it most definitely and rapidly becomes too hot. In such conditions reptiles require little basking to sufficiently warm their bodies for the activities of the day, with even night-time temperatures often persisting in the mid-twenties. The yellow stripes and green tail of the little Danford's Lizard, a relative of our own Common Lizard, but known only from Turkey and Greece, will far more likely be seen darting over rocks and around tree roots, rather than across the sun-baked open ground.

The ground beneath the cover of pines every so often yields to the shallow ravines of stony streams, or even river beds, bereft of water. They did flow with the winter and spring rains but now they look as if water might never wash over the rocks again. The water will flow again, but for now they appear every bit as parched as the land around them. The forest plants made the most of the earlier time of plenty before the summer set its influence indiscriminately throughout the forest. Stands of yellowed Syrian Thistle line the paths, now offering up barely even a scattering of colour, where previously they would have daubed the wayside mauve. The shrubby Chaste Trees throw up the odd purple spike, but they too have largely done flowering, and the clumps of Mediterranean Spurge dotted among the boulders have long since given up any sign of their spring flowers but leave an echo of a vernal resurgence that would have delivered the same sense of growth and eager life as in any British woodland. The pine forest still welcomes and is a pleasure to be within, but it looks so very thirsty. Water is present here – the spring-bearing limestone sees to that – but it is in sparse supply.

This is nothing new of course. Turkey's Mediterranean regions have always seen summer temperatures peak around the high thirties, often tipping over 40. Even at higher altitude it may be only a few degrees cooler. But this is the way of things. This is how the pine forests of the Olympos-beydağları National Park get through the year. It will rain and it will do so a lot, but 90% of its 1,000 millimetres (40 inches – about the same amount as parts of eastern Scotland) will fall between October to March, leaving the later spring and summer months typically dry and hot. But even in the heat and dryness of August it still maintains the hum of life and not only in the more literal sense of the untiring drone of the cicada.

With its scattering of natural springs, there is always water to be found and to these the forest centres its attentions. In this instance, an apparently rather aged, vaguely ornate concrete structure, perhaps a metre and half high, manifests the running water of an underground spring, via a pipe a couple of centimetres wide. Behind it, surrounded by pine trees, is what might initially be described as a large puddle. It is shallow, algae filled and shaded, and only some six or so metres wide and slightly less across. It does not appear enticing. Certainly not like the shore of some lily-strewn lake fringed with lush green foliage. It seems wholly unremarkable: merely the seepage of a natural spring dribbling to the surface to become a rather foetid, unfulfilled puddle beneath the shade of the forest trees.

Although not always presenting an engaging face, the workings of nature can so rarely be fully judged on surface value. This seemingly swampy and uninspiring accumulation of water is not stagnant, as its appearance might suggest. How could it be? It is filled with fresh, clean spring water, filtered through the porous rocks that lift these forests a thousand metres above sea level. Walk on past and this initial impression might persist. Sit a while beside it and instead a deeper sense of the presence of permanent freshwater in a hot, dry landscape will become keenly experienced. There is no definable boundary between the trees that stand in its immediate vicinity and those further away, but an air of place within place fills the scene around it and nudges the perception of the senses.

Understated it may be, but it is very much, in its way, a special place.

Its virtues are not immediately obvious. The willowherb emerging from the shallows seem still, as still as the water amid which they stand and the branches of the canopy overhead. And then a movement diverts the eye and leads to another, then another and another: a pale, pastel blue insect lifting from its perch and within moments drawing the attention of others. They are dragonflies, male Small Skimmers vying for territory, dashing low across the water and meeting each other in brief, wing-clattering conflicts and, with disputes temporarily settled, returning to their own private vigils. A male and a dull yellow female, already joined, keep a low profile. The puddle comes to life...and becomes a pool.

As the world at the water's surface enlivens, so too does the realm of the canopy overhead. The woods, previously filled only by the relentless buzz of the cicada, are now sprinkled with the quiet twitter of birds. Similar to a British broad-leaved wood at the same time of year, the forest had seemingly been near devoid of bird sound, until the happening upon of a mixed flock (or indeed them happening upon me). The pool is a magnet to them, drawn to it by the promise of water to drink and of tiny insects to eat. All of a sudden the branches above are filled with Great, Coal and Long-tailed Tits, familiarly flocking together with their breeding season over. Familiar too, is the presence of other birds among their number. A Chiffchaff, its pale underparts flushed with the fresh yellow of its autumn plumage, descends to pick minuscule, unseen (to me) creatures from the muddy fringes. A pair of Short-toed Treecreepers examines the trunks of the pine, attentively spiralling upwards in search of those insects that seek shelter in the fissures of the bark. A Kruper's Nuthatch, a rather smaller version of the widespread Eurasian Nuthatch and sporting a reddish-brown breast patch, flits onto the side of a tree with its roots set into the pool and edges its way tentatively downwards to slake a pinenut-induced thirst.

Other dragonflies appear. A Southern Skimmer, a lighter blue and larger than the Small, chances a claim over a piece of the pool to the chagrin of the already incumbent others. A female Ruddy Darter takes up a perch between bouts of ovipositing, laying her eggs by dabbing her abdomen into the water while still on the wing. A movement amid the emergent willowherb reveals the bronzed-green of a damselfly – an Eastern Willow Spreadwing.

The pool and its pine trees, so apparently lifeless at first glance, are now captivating with this unceasing flux of life. The birds, the dragonflies and others too. A Cardinal, the largest of the European fritillaries, swoops down impressively among the trees, settling a while at the edge of the pool, perhaps to take minerals from the damp ground fringing its edge, before fluttering up and settling among the lower branches. Oriental Hornets come and go, requiring mud for nest building, constructing these perhaps against a tree or some huge rock. An old livestock trough – looking derelict, but evidently still water tight – provides a residence for a solitary Marsh Frog, the pool and its environs offering a summer sanctuary until the return of damper, cooler times. A knobbly protrusion jutting from a boulder across the pool turns out to be the head of a Starred Agama, a thick set, bulldog of a lizard, enjoying the tempered warmth and dampness beneath the trees.

But, it seems that, except for the ubiquitous cicadas and sun-craving grasshoppers, the pool draws all within its influence. The birds for which it comprises an essential component of their landscape, the dragonflies that must visit it to complete their life cycles and even the reptiles that at some point need to drink from it. And finally, the human observer pulled, in a different way, but no less inexorably towards it: transfixed, enthralled and so pleasantly surprised.

Part 2

Shifting Perspectives

Shifting Perspectives

It is too tempting here, not to begin with that age-old saying: 'Things aren't always as they seem', a phrase that would indeed go some way to describing the context of this whole book. For the multi-faceted and seemingly boundless depths of nature this rings especially true. So rare must it be for anyone to set eyes on anything for the first time and see it in its entirety. There will always be a layer to be figuratively stripped away, a new strand of investigation to be followed along with and the new discoveries that may flow in its wake. The challenge before us here is one of a more open mind and the subtlety of our perception. Then the familiar places and circumstances might yield other layers of life, laid out on the edges of our human senses, but always present should we be inclined to adjust the focus of our attentions.

There may be few better ways to begin to explain this to a weather-obsessed nation than, indeed, the weather. Not that we are necessarily obsessed by it. Certainly, many a gap in conversation is filled by our observations of it and often as small talk – a way of passing something more than just the time of day with someone whose acquaintance we are happy to be making. It does, nevertheless, provide the topic for discussion of genuine interest. We talk a lot about it as we get to see so very much of it.

Take a rainy day. A rainy June day and a blank page. Even if it does briefly stop raining, the greyness still looms. The conveyor belt of low stratus clouds gives the impression of pausing only to gather new impetus for another bout of dreary precipitation. A rainy day in June can dampen the mood as much as anything, yet it may be better thought of as the time for the spring's final ascent to its crescendo and the onset of summer.

June expects. The hues of buttercup-strewn meadows require the sun's rays across their swathes and the crane's-bill pinks are lifted by them; the orchid spikes spire more proudly towards the faultless, clear blue. In place of the blue, though, is a sluggishly swirling firmament of shifting shades of grey. Teasing when their opacity yields enough to allow the sun to glow dully through their veil, before thickening and seeming to squeeze some of the light of late spring from the day to achieve that singular, heavy dullness of impending rain.

Looking from the window onto such a scene for inspiration – how is a page ever to be filled? Even the Woodpigeons would seem to reflect the writer's mood, sat hunched and soaked on their perches, the hoped-for cover sought from the leafy branches around them having proved quite ineffective, except maybe for no more than the first few minutes of rainfall. The Swifts that earlier had slashed their trails overhead have out-flown the worst of the weather front for fairer skies and more profitable foraging. The thin branches of the birch tree are disturbed, not by any acrobatics of aphid-hungry Blue Tit but by the falling of incessant rain, the pliable twigs yielding obediently to each impact. So forceful are the torrents that the tits and the other garden familiars have gone for cover, with apparently rather more success than the conspicuously drenched pigeons; size, to be fair, is not on the side of the latter.

At least we can take some solace from the fact that things would have to be much worse to match the June of 1879. Richard Jefferies, writing on the sixth month of that year, recalled a longest day in England's southern counties with a morning full of rain and a wind in the evening that "*howled down the chimneys like a true winter blast*". He told of a Midsummer Day that was "*wild and rough*". It was one that brought morning rain and heavy afternoon showers; thunder, hail and "*rough gusts of wind sending the leaves spinning away*". Sure enough, back in this 21st-century June day, hail storms have not needed contending with and the gales have not ravaged the trees, but it is very wet and very grey.

Only the imagination will see the damselflies that sparkled vivid blues and deep reds in yesterday's sunshine and that now shelter unseen among the nearby plants. With them, and just as patiently waiting out the rain, are the Holly Blue butterflies that skipped along the hedge and the bumblebees that twitched the garden geraniums. It is our imagination that sees them, and assumes that they are there, along with all those other small creatures of sunny June days. For every diminutive denizen that adds to the throng in the sunshine, it is apparent that there are at least an equal number of nooks or crannies to conceal them during the unseasonal storms. So complete is their absence during the one instance and so ubiquitous and swift is their reappearance in another, seeming almost to magically materialise from thin air when the clouds draw away from the sun.

With our attention drawn to things we cannot even see, perhaps this dull and wet late-spring day is much less dreary for the knowledge of them. Perhaps we might be more inclined to watch the patterns of the raindrops on the surface of the pond, each rippling the image of the towering trees and elegantly unfurled Yellow Iris blooms and mingling them into a shimmering, viscous collage of shade and colour and undefined shapes. We might watch for a while, entranced for few moments by this play of water on water. From the palette of the rhythmically falling rain and the predictability of its cause and effect on the water's surface, a satisfyingly chaotic composition, is produced.

Just as they are by the heat of the sun, each sense is enlivened by the rain. The smell of it as it soaks the dry earth and conjures the odour of greenness from all around, and fills the woods with that sweet smell of decay – the scent of the processes that drives the ecology of these rich and diverse places. The feeling of the relief it gives from the cloying heat of rising and sustained humidity. The gleam of the rain-soaked understorey across the verdurous woodland floor. The sound of it as it patters on the numberless leaves with equally numberless raindrops – the sound of replenishment. These are all aspects of freshness and as such can be relished. I fondly remember once camping in a relatively quiet corner of a field busy with other campers and surrounded by a woodland of grand beech trees, old oaks and the assorted holly, rowan, hazel and hawthorn striving to fill the spaces underneath. We lay on our stomachs at the entrance of our small tent and watched the rain drive down before us and listened to its relentlessness on the fabric over our heads. It rained for what seemed like ages and we lay for ages, watching, listening and imagining the silence of the wood waiting behind the din of the falling rain.

With the inconveniences of the rain, we are inclined to hanker for the sun and its warmth while forgetting, at least for a while, the rigours that that too might exert on the things in our surroundings. Yes, the sunlight draws the colours of nature more forcibly towards our gaze, but so too does the spring rain, albeit with more subtlety. Perhaps not with the dazzle of bright light, but instead in the deepening green of the slaked foliage and the inwardly intensified colours of the blooms among the branches and the blades. The buttercups in the meadow will still glow even in the dulled light beneath a cloud-laden sky and the crane's-bills and orchids will be instead lifted and revitalised by the moistened soil at their roots. The gardens, the woods and the grasslands – anywhere where the green of leaves predominates – replete from the rain, will just give slightly an outward heave, burgeoning to fill the spaces and to make the most of the weather at hand with its opportunity for exuberance and the promise of dryer times ahead.

Whilst the rain hijacks a late spring day and robs us, at least for a time, of those summery joys – the buzz, the warmth, the colour enriched – even this can still provide the words to fill a page. Words can still flow in the rivulets that chase down the windowpane...from the simple idea of the things of the season consumed and concealed by their environs and the promise of their prompt return. Inspiration might unfold to occupy the widening circles of ripples expanding. There is surely pleasure to be taken from the knowledge of the sated earth and the quenching of the landscape.

The potential for such a shifting of our perspective is essentially continuous. From the weather and the landscapes over which it prevails, to the tiniest components beneath and within. Imagine a visit to a new place. From where you stand, a green pasture slopes down towards distant trees and a winding ribbon of rushing river water glimpsed in between them. The land heaves up steeply behind, first through scattered Rowan trees and a miniature forest of bracken before gradually giving way to a sweep of heather and moorland grasses smothering the highest ground, absent only where the craggy exposures of rock is visible here and there – the bones of the landscape bared. Looking on downstream, past the subtly changing textures of the riparian trees, of the oak and willow, alder and scattered thorn, the flanking incline of the land edges back, the river divides as it rounds the bend, around an island of trees and fern clad boulders. The trees that lined the river upstream now begin to funnel out into a wood, taking advantage of the yielding relief in the topography, filling the flat ground beside the river's course and ascending the valley slopes, so that even after the river has bent out of sight the valley side behind presents a curtain of satisfying green.

This is where it begins. The point made, if you like, in the simplest of terms. A landscape full of variety and texture, endlessly pleasing to the eye. The rushing river, the bare stones, the inviting concealment of the woods – triggers for the imagination. And it is the imagination that takes us further in. Deeper into the woods and closer to the Treecreeper spiralling the boles and the spired foxgloves amidst the sunny breaks in the canopy. Along the banks of the river and the glimpses of trout surfacing for water-trapped insects and the whirr of dragonfly wings. Among the heather on the high ground and whistle and twitter of small birds – the hidden pipits and Wheatear.

When the imagination wavers, the objects of our fascination carry us deeper still. What might be those unfortunate insects that meet their watery, fishy end? What does the Dipper pursue when it submerges to defy the river's current? What was that movement that darted at the edge of my vision and briefly diverted my attention from the fritillary butterflies sunning themselves on the nectar-rich bramble blossom? And so it continues, onwards and inwards. By considering the "*richness and structure*" in a single handful of soil, Edward O. Wilson takes us in his book *Biophilia: The human bond with other species* towards the nth degree:

> "*When the soil-and-litter clump is progressively magnified…specks of dead leaf expand into mountain ranges and canyons, soil particles become heaps of boulders. A droplet of moisture trapped between root hairs grows into an underground lake, surrounded by a three-dimensional swamp of moistened humus.*"

Our heightened focus need not, however, be concerned only with looking inwards, but might instead require just an alteration of our perspective. A different way of looking, focus perhaps, merely heightened than intensified, concerned not only with the finer detail of the component parts but also with their interrelatedness, their unfolding within a landscape.

This can be experienced anywhere there is life. I offer in the chapters that follow a few personal experiences which have brought this very clearly to my attention. They were not instances that were especially remarkable, at least not on the face of them, yet they did indeed prove in some way remarkable, enough to be recounted now. At the time, these experiences did not seem to be any more remarkable than those normally gleaned in terms of inherent fascination to a naturalist. But, it was on reflection that they came to hold a greater significance, when I allowed my imagination to make firmer those aspects only hinted at by the physical things in front of me.

So much of nature is beyond the comprehension of our other senses. I have on occasion, while watching a fox slinking along a hedge, around trees and along tracks through the grass and with its nose to the ground, tried to contemplate the world of smells that it exists and interacts in. I tried to imagine how it might perceive the trails of scent that I fancy to be like the faintest, vaporous wisps that cling as the ribbons of a morning mist do, to form invisible pathways traced along the hedgerows, through the woods and criss-crossing the open country. Of course, as intriguing as all this may sound, I don't expect I come remotely close to seeing the reality of things through the efforts of my imaginings – the real truth of how an animal 'sees' the scents in its olfactory landscape – but it is nevertheless an interesting exercise in remembering the limitations of our own perceptions and perhaps also some of their hidden potential.

A Bumblebee's Eye View

Bumblebees in Britain have not been having a very happy time of things over recent decades. Our modern agricultural methods and development activities have done them no favours at all. A single colony would need plenty of flowers on which to forage, with the workers of some species travelling up to 400 metres from the nest in search of suitable foraging, that is nectar and pollen sources. An arc traced 400 metres out from a central point covers an area, the theoretical maximum home range of a bumblebee colony, of very nearly 40 hectares! Such swathes of continuous flower-rich habitats are a very rare thing in this day and age which, as a consequence, is bad news for our bumblebees. There are 24 species on the British list. Several of these are still common, but a number of others are suffering significant decline, including some of the more numerous and widespread species. Two have become extinct as British species during recent times.

Despite their great popularity and familiarity, do we perhaps take the bumblebee a little for granted? That we can allow some to become rare and even go extinct might suggest that we do. Given the vital role that bumblebees play in the pollination of human food crops, we do this almost as much to our disadvantage as to theirs. We do rather accept the bumblebee – prodding among the garden geraniums, drifting purposefully among municipal flowers at the local park, or busily inspecting the pink-purple globes of red clover by the grassy verge – as something taken for granted. The town bumblebee is not an unusual thing, and even away from the countryside most of us very likely spend a great deal of time in their company and are rarely very far from them at all, especially given that they may roam so widely. Wherever a good concentration of nectar-rich flowers is to be found, so too might bumblebees occur in good numbers, as much a truism to the garden as it is to the flowery meadow.

Even though a naturalist, I have to admit, to my shame, that I have not previously given the bumblebees their due attention. I have not ignored them as such but rather accepted them as a part of the world closer to the peripheries of my experience. Not ignored, but yes – alas taken them for granted. This, I decided, was something in need of remedy and so I took it upon myself to begin studying the bumblebee community inhabiting a small area of land in south Essex. Even though only about two hectares in area, the site encompassed a mixture of different habitats: half a hectare of hay meadow and various other pockets of grassland, a developing woodland and scattering of mature trees, developing scrub and thick hedgerows and a couple of ponds.

I intended that the survey should ascertain what species of bumblebee used the site and to observe something of their habits throughout the year. It was also my place of work, so putting in the recording hours was – I hoped – not going to be too much of a problem. I wanted to learn something of their foraging preferences and their patterns of activity throughout the season and to understand more about their life cycles. To this end I decided, given the limited area of the site, that I would attempt to perform total bumblebee counts and note the chosen source of forage for each one as I saw it. But how could I ensure that I saw each bee present at a given time? Not all would necessarily be on the move and hence obvious. And how could I be sure that as I counted one insect I had not counted it already? Bumblebees of the same species would appear pretty much identical to each other. Of course, I couldn't make guarantees on either. I would just have to assume that a thorough and systematic approach to walking the site during the daily surveys would minimise the risk of non-observation and double counting. That way the counts made would at the very least be representative on a day-to-day, year-to-year basis.

During the first year, after 110 individual surveys and a bit more than 5,000 individual bee sightings later, I had gathered the data with which to form a picture of the bumblebees on site. Even a single year's observation provides an insight. Through subsequent years, the image would only be further enhanced, with differences to ponder and new anomalies to consider. I had never really undertaken such a task before, singling out a single group of organisms and immersing myself in the nuances of their behaviour and activities. Evaluating the data at the end of the year, I was intrigued, excited even, about what these might reveal. What I didn't quite expect, however, was to not only obtain a deeper insight into the creatures of my study, as I had initially intended, but also to experience a change in the way I looked at the whole place. Not that I gained literally 'a bumblebee's eye view', rather they offered me a different starting point from which to explore and experience the whole natural history of the site; a subtle but comprehensive shift of perspective. I was drawn further apart from a more typically anthropocentric take on things and closer to a view of nature from within itself. Many of the reasons for all of this seem almost too obvious to make mention of, but within this lies much of the meaning and fascination of the entire experience. I was a good way from the cutting edge of bumblebee research, but the insights I gained had a genuine and gently profound effect on me.

Of the bumblebees themselves, even before I met them in the field, and as mentioned in Ted Benton's excellent book *The Bumblebees of Essex*, a great deal of what is so fascinating about their behaviour takes place within the concealment of the nest. The story, most of the time, is centred around the queen. Unlike honey bees, a bumblebee colony breaks up by the autumn. Having mated before the season's end, it is only the new queens produced during the current year that will survive the winter in hibernation. She emerges in the spring and immediately seeks nectar with which to replenish her now exhausted fat and sugar reserves. She must feed, not only to sustain herself but also in order for her ovaries to develop and to begin producing eggs to start her colony.

She will be eager also to search for a place to make her nest, the location of which will depend on the species. The likes of Buff-tailed and White-tailed Bumblebees, for example, usually nest underground, quite often in old mouse holes. The Early-nesting Bumblebee, in contrast, is more inclined to nest off the ground, among the bottom of bushes, in tree holes or even old bird nests. Carder bees, one of which is the familiar orange-haired Common Carder Bee, usually nest on or just beneath the ground and take their names from their behaviour of carding, or combing moss with which to cover the nest. Within the nest the first small clutch of eggs hatches into maggot-like grubs that ultimately pupate into workers (infertile females). These then assume the tasks of building the waxen cells for the nest and of searching for food, leaving the queen to concentrate her efforts on producing young. More workers are produced, and later in the summer males and fertile females (the new queens). They mate and the wheel turns full circle.

So, yes, a great deal of the bumblebee colony's life is enacted out of human sight, but what is visible can be enlightening, if only in the simplicity of its ways. During the inaugural year of my survey, the season began on February 23rd, with the sighting of a single Early-nesting Bumblebee queen, closely followed by a Buff-tailed Bumblebee queen (perhaps the most familiar of all our bumblebees) three days later. A sighting of a single, hardy Buff-tailed queen marked the season's close on November 17th. The intervening nine months revealed the ebb and flow of life and activity, with the bees responding to the changes taking place throughout the period. Changes that were sometimes more abrupt, with the ascent of summer and the reliable unpredictability of the climate, at other times more subliminal – the more subtle drift of progress and process that operates throughout the countryside.

Activity built slowly into the beginning of May, numbers toing and froing between just single insects (but never none at all as it turned out) when the days of spring rain kept their activity to a minimum (bumblebees really don't like the rain) to rarely as many as twenty. Then the early workers began to appear in numbers. First the Early-nesting Bumblebee, living true to their name, later as the days progressed the Buff-tailed and Common Carder Bee. From then on there seemed little holding them back. The daily totals rose steeply and in the matter of two or three weeks soared twice during late May and early June to near on 200.

Quite suddenly the peak of activity had been attained, but the subsequent decrease in sightings took place more gradually. Numbers on site would fluctuate, sometimes wildly. Between those two high counts in May and June numbers halved before rising again. Such peaks and troughs were repeated throughout the year, demonstrating, I assumed, how colonies make use of wide areas, coming and going in number as the foraging opportunities changed with the lives of the plants that moved through their own life cycles. It is easy to think that if there are flowers suitable for bumblebees to collect pollen from, then gather they will, with little regard for the species that provide them with their precious resources. The bees, though, very much seemed to have their favourites. A fifth of all foraging observations related to Russian Comfrey, the most visited plant during the course of the year. Other plants would be to some extent rebuffed, or even totally ignored, in favour of the small, drooping pink blooms of the sought-after comfrey. But as its flowering began to drop off, so the bees were more inclined to forage elsewhere. There is a definite economy in how bumblebees forage, with individual workers concentrating their efforts on a single plant species at a time. And different bees would have different favourites. The Red-tailed

Bumblebee, for example, much preferred Greater Bird's-foot Trefoil when it was in flower to anything else. It in fact showed a clear preference to yellow flowers in general with more than half of foraging visits to the blooms of this colour. Male White-tailed Bumblebees on the other hand appeared rather fond of white flowers, with White Clover and Hogweed particularly well liked.

So not only did I witness the slight changes in the behaviour of the bees themselves but also how the wider landscape influenced their movement, thus finding myself considering the lives of other things, in this instance the plants, in a different light, not just in relation to the bees but in their own right. The insects were marking the subtlest of changes within their environment than my own observation could not hope to appreciate. This finer detail of the growth and cycles of wild flowers visited were in effect lifted towards my attention and that of other life also. I would find my eyes focusing into and on the spaces and things in a figurative sense in-between where I would normally look.

For example I knew the Small Copper butterfly well from the site. Their caterpillars feed on the Common Sorrel that grows throughout the grassy places, among the clovers and vetches that the bumblebees sought. But now I could appreciate some of their own peculiarities; their favourite corners and liking for the nectar of Fleabane flowers. There were also the Small Skipper butterflies that buzzed restlessly about the grasses in number, but which I would often see nectaring with the Common Carder Bee on the little mauve columns of Tufted Vetch.

A more intent scouring of each and every corner of the site revealed the presence of others that might more often than not have gone undetected. The Field Grasshopper seemed to have increased over the last couple of years, especially among the flower-rich sward near the ponds where the massed knapweeds, trefoils and clovers lured bumblebees of all species. There was a small species of longhorn beetle that I would only ever see on Dog Rose blooms. The crab spider – *Misumena* – was far more numerous than I had ever previously realised, changing colour to blend in with yellow or white flowers and pouncing on the unwary – bumblebee worker in search of pollen or nectar.

I learnt more about the movements of the resident Adder population, so often an elusive animal. They liked short grass in the corner of the hay meadow where Common Carder Bee queens would be seen about the Ground Ivy in spring and which scrambled in the lea of a large oak. Often I would find them basking in the morning sunshine, in a clearing among the Blackthorn scrub whose copious white flowers provided such an important source of forage after the catkins had gone over on the Sallow. And I would need to watch my step too along the grassy fringe of the new wood where Wild Cherry coloured the greening spring crowns.

In such a way the whole place, which I knew very well before, was being elevated further, more cohesively into my awareness. I imagined a kind of aerial view with the trails of the living things plotted throughout; the briefly crossing paths and the fleeting overlapping of lives, or those entangled and inextricably entwined with one and other – pollen makers and pollinators, predator and prey.

Of all such incidental observations it was perhaps those insects that mimicked the bumblebees which, if only within the context of the survey, particularly came to the fore. Mimicry is something that numerous species make use of, not only of bumblebees but also honeybees and wasps. Honeybees, for instance, have as mimic the Dronefly, a very common hoverfly, whilst the Hornet has the large and rather impressive black and yellow hoverfly *Volucella zonaria*. Potential predators may well give you a wider berth if you resemble something that they know might sting them. Various flies make use of such deception, as does the common species of solitary bee

Anthophora plumipes. There are even moths that use the same ploy, for example the so-called Bee Hawk-moths and a rare species of rove beetle, *Emus hirtus*, as well.

Among the best disguised, however, is the hoverfly *Volucella bombylans*, the so-called Bumblebee Hoverfly. It is one of five British species of *Volucella* hoverflies, all of which mimic bumblebees or wasps. All, except one, live in close association with the nests of such insects. Eggs will be laid within the nests where the resultant grubs feed as scavengers on the collected debris at the bottom of the nest or even as a parasite of the host larvae. I had seen *V. bombylans* on the site before but only now realised that they were actually quite common and became a most familiar late-spring sight, zipping about in the sunshine and always close to the hedgerows and scrub. I noted them in two different forms. One was clothed with yellow, black and white hairs so as to resemble the various species of bumblebee with similar arrangements of colours, such as the Buff-tailed, White-tailed and Garden Bumblebees. The other form took the appearance of the Red-tailed Bumblebee with the tip of the abdomen similarly adorned with bright orange hairs. It was the former that were more numerous. I never saw the other, much rarer form that is clothed in the orange-brown hairs akin to the Common Carder Bee.

But the most convincing of all bumblebee mimics are other species of bumblebee – the cuckoo bumblebees. These are parasites of which there are six species in Britain and have forgone the requirement for a social lifestyle, parasitizing the nests and the collaborative life cycle of social species in order to complete their own. Each 'cuckoo' has its particular, or at least most commonly used host, to which it will in many instances bear an impressive resemblance. The female cuckoo will seek out and enter a nest of its host species. Initially she has to resist the attacks of the incumbent workers alarmed at this invader in their midst. She hides herself among the paraphernalia of the nesting materials until she no longer attracts the attention of the workers, perhaps because she has taken on the scent of her new surroundings. Then she assumes control of the nest. The host queen is subdued, sometimes even killed, and the cuckoo begins to lay her own eggs. She does not produce a worker brood as she has no need of one. The host workers continue their foraging labours, now for the benefit of this next generation of male and female cuckoos. She may even destroy the host eggs when sufficient workers are available to rear her family.

The endeavours of the cuckoo bumblebees may not exactly be endearing but are really very fascinating. They provide a window on other such treacheries taking place all around the countryside, of nature taking all opportunities and exploring all avenues of survival. Brood parasitism seems particularly prevalent among bees. The dozens of mining bees that perforated an area of bare clay soil by the drive had their attendant, wasp-like nomad bees that take advantage of the pre-stocked burrows, as well as the bumblebee mimicking bee-flies whose own young feed on those of the host species. Leaf-cutter bees meet with a similar problem with their own parasites, *Coelioxys* sp., as do the mason bees whose clay-constructed cells attract the attentions of the cuckoos of the genus *Stelis*. Treacherous to the human mind, but part of the mechanics of the balance and fine tuning of the natural world.

My survey revealed three cuckoo bumblebee species to be present. Much the most common was the Southern Cuckoo Bumblebee that invades the nests of Buff-tailed Bumblebees. Another was the Red-tailed Cuckoo Bumblebee, a superb mimic of the Red-tailed Bumblebee and something of a minor rarity. Lastly, there was the Forest Cuckoo Bumblebee, parasites of the Early-nesting Bumblebee. I discovered the nests of Buff-tailed and Red-tailed Bumblebees and the workers of the Early-nesting Bumblebee occurred in such high numbers as to suggest they may also had nested on site, but undiscovered. It was not very surprising that the three cuckoo bumblebees found are parasites of these eusocial species.

The survey continued for three quarters of the year. I estimated that I had walked more than 100 kilometres around an area of just a couple of hectares looking for bumblebees. In total, I saw eleven species, all mentioned in this chapter. Some of them were quite rare, with regular sightings of Red-tailed Cuckoo Bumblebee and Brown-banded Carder Bee, plus one sighting of the recent UK coloniser, the Tree Bumblebee; the last were destined to take up residency in the area, with frequent sightings of workers during the subsequent years of the survey. I noted how they came and went as part of their use of a wider home range. I observed their foraging preferences and how they changed allegiance to different flowers throughout the year according to availability. How the bumblebees would pretty much ignore the plentiful yellow Fleabane blooms and copious white flower heads of Wild Carrot while the assorted hoverflies, soldier beetles and butterflies feasted; had I been studying hoverflies I might well have been asking the question as to why they seemed to be indifferent to the vetches and trefoils. I observed in a subtly different way than before how interactions take place and connections are made throughout the wider environment at the unseen and often unapparent whim of those that comprised it.

Thus, through this window into the more intricate workings of the place, during my study of the bumblebees I came to look upon it in a different way. This included the role in the scheme of things of some of the other insects that brush wings, however fleetingly, with the bumblebees. The communities of flowers, the gradation and continuity between habitats; the subtleties of nature we take for granted, that is if we come to notice them in the first place. The willow tree and its spring blossom, the spread of clover among the hay meadow, the percolation of colour from the shadow of the trees of the Ground Ivy edging into the spring sunlight. Even the cushions of moss, providers of nesting material that thrive amid the damper areas of sward assumed a slightly different place in my casual attention. The cycles and patterns of growth and flowering of a community of plants and the subtleties of the steady flux of life and change. How nature always provides, sometimes only just and often in profusion, but always without waver. How first the willows crucially yielded their catkins, to be followed by the white hedgerow swathes of Blackthorn blossom. And just as the Blackthorn waned, so the Pear blossom appeared on the branches and by the time those blooms were lost to the greening foliage the succession of wild flowers among the grasses was well under way. The flowering and growth of plants – such a simple chain of events, but one that underpins the existence of so many other living organisms and yet so taken for granted and maybe too obvious to be readily appreciated. It is against such simple rhythms that life flourishes and, to us, captivates. There were always flowers, even if only the scattered Dandelions, that helped fill the gaps while the spring gathered pace, and there were always bumblebees. This is a state of affairs we should strive to maintain.

With the survey continuing into subsequent years, such awareness deepened. With comparison possible, the quiet surging and abating of life throughout the seasons was brought into a clearer focus, which only sharpened with further time and study. The studies began to reveal how the many variables that surround them can change, however slightly, the shape of bumblebee activity. During the second year, sharp May frosts postponed the expected steep rise in bumblebee numbers towards the end of the month, but when they did finally climb they did so higher than before, almost as if the unseasonal inclemencies stiffened their resolve. In spite of this frost-induced curtailing of proceedings, the timing of the peak counts for that and the previous survey coincided within a day;

there was a sense that the bees were making up for lost time. This was something reflected in a number of the individual species. They captured perfectly the mood of a spring restrained and then unfurled in a festival of activity.

As well as the excitement of sighting a very rare Shrill Carder Bee queen, the following year brought an unusually 'summery' spring. The consequently advanced flowering of many of the plants served to alter the foraging patterns of the bumblebees, if only for the simple reason that well-used flowers during the previous April were shunned for others that would normally not have been in bloom and hence available to the bees. Some species, however, were more stubborn in adhering to their life cycles. With the bumblebee's eye view it was more obvious that the Greater Bird's-foot Trefoil stuck rather firmly to its usual flowering time, while the Common Bird's-foot Trefoil flushed early with its rich yellow blooms. Similarly, with the Red Clover that daubed the meadow sward with colour well before the grasses had towered over them and the first Knapweed flowers appearing in time to overlap with the last of the year's ground ivy.

The warm spring brought about a predictable advance also in the numbers of several of the bumblebee species. But the curve that might be imagined to graphically represent their activity failed to show that steep rise through the earlier half of spring towards the abrupt explosion of activity in May or June, but rather a steady and sustained increase in activity. There seemed no need to catch up on time lost, as there was during the cold snap the year before. Thus this particular season allowed a quiet appreciation of the warmth and sunshine that filled those spring months, giving a firmer impression of assured endeavour that we so often associate with the 'busy' bumblebee. Once again they encapsulated the mood of the wider countryside. A countryside perhaps, that as a whole and, after the initial surging of the spring from its winter clutches, felt almost surprised at the unseasonal turn in the climate before proceeding to fill the air as best it could with the buzz of a summer yet to arrive. With a similar air of sustained diligence and with the arrival of the summer proper, the peak of activity proved rather lower than the two previous years, nearly 25% lower in fact. But rather than the sharp late-spring rise and the gradual drawn-out decline in numbers into the autumn, the peaks on the graph would cast a shape of sustained activity – quality, if you like, rather than quantity. It made the outline a little like some flat-topped hulk of a heather-capped hill instead of a soaring mountain ridge; more of a Pen-y-Ghent than a Pen-y-Fan.

Such changes in behaviour, which may be subtle and unlikely to add a huge amount to the greater knowledge of bumblebees in general, nevertheless to me emphasised the fine detail of the oscillating rhythms of life and environment that I might otherwise have failed to experience. Had I not been watching them closely I would have remained unaware of any year-to-year anomalies. I would have noted that they appeared by late winter and disappeared by mid-autumn, and the time in between would have had its bumblebees as normal. I very likely would have been wholly ignorant of the changing patterns contained within.

Around the fulcrum of the bumblebees' presence the whole place appeared to pivot. A new angle from which to observe the interactions of organisms and habitat, the weather and the seasons, beyond the more obvious agents of light and dark, warm and cold. The bumblebees' experience of a landscape is one that is perfectly in tune with everything occurring all around them. To the likely extent that they are not even aware of much of what takes place beyond the 'bumblebee universe' but instead responding to the patterns and rhythms with a kind of instinctive honesty that regrettably seems to have drifted far away from much of our human existence. The life of the bumblebee fits in with the flush, flower and fall of plants, and its life cycle takes place in spite of most other organisms in their midst, as indeed these others do of them. Beyond the obvious influence of the passing seasons, the easy heave and swell of life comes and goes with a barely tangible effect on the organisms that comprise it. As the variables of their environment shift through their own cycles, so the lives of the bumblebees alter without effort and barely a notice to match the changes. Like a raft of Eider floating offshore on the benign waves of an ebbing tide, they all just ride the gentle rise and fall while scarcely noticing the movement.

I could choose any point within that same web of life that strikes off from those paths worn by the bumblebees, select a different fulcrum and begin from there. Like a spider's web illumined in a sunlit woodland glade, the whole place seeming centred around it, radiating from those silken spokes and extrapolating into a greater web of ever-growing depth and complexity. Nothing lives in isolation, and my bumblebees represent just one of so many analogies. The Goat Willow, for example, so crucial to the freshly emerged spring queens. Bumblebees aside, our native willows (of which there are 19 species) are, ecologically speaking, vastly productive, with more than 600 different species of invertebrate known to rely upon or utilise them. What patterns and threads of life would radiate from them? The bumblebees are just one breath of life that brushes their boughs as the year passes by. Or maybe an investigation into the distribution of leguminous plants (clovers, vetches and such like – all members of the family Fabaceae) on the site, important providers not just of nectar and pollen to bumblebees but sustenance to a host of insect life – butterflies, moths and beetles – and not to mention their intriguing symbiosis with nitrogen-fixing bacteria that obtain nutrients from soil to be taken up by their host in exchange for energy from the plant. Or the dragonfly nymphs that thrive in profusion within the ponds around which the riotous assemblage of bumblebee-attracting wild flowers blazed during the summer, the adults gracing the summer air with their exciting beauty. The voraciously predatory nymphs depend on the productivity of an often extravagantly adapted community of creatures, the adults assuming their part of a fascinating lifecycle and linking together the worlds of water and air. Each, like the bumblebees, would bring the connectivity of nature into a clearer awareness. We are not so much singling something out as being necessarily more remarkable than anything else within its surroundings than temporarily occupying their place as a platform for our own experiences.

This, then, is how a survey focussed on bumblebees can echo through the whole of the habitats and landscape in which they live. How they can become analogous of nature's rhythms within rhythms; the circles within circles that in turn overlap with other circles within circles. This is how the bumblebee might alter the way one looks at the world, or rather how one might encourage others to re-look at what is around them. One could choose anything and be similarly engrossed and drawn deeply into the hidden realms of nature and given a glimpse of a different view. Yet all the while, you may still be contented to merely sit, enjoy the busy hum of diligent insects and look upon the merging colours of textures of a landscape and its habitats and imagine what wonders reside within.

The World Afloat

Something peculiar happens when you are on board a boat. A peculiar, but very fundamental and almost unnoticeable change. Once again, a shifting of perspective, but significantly in this instance, not one which is exclusively ours but which encompasses the world immediately around us. Such a shift will, of course, take place in a most obvious way. Clearly, to not be standing on a bank or beach but within the scene that you would otherwise be looking out onto will naturally result in a different perspective on things. From a rowing boat on the surface of the river the banks loom rather higher than we might expect, so used, as we are, to viewing the water surface 30 centimetres beneath our feet and another metre and half or so below the level of our eyes. Looking from some offshore position back towards the land and we can better fix our distance within the mind than when gazing from the shore and out towards the horizon across the endless, rippling sheet of the sea.

By taking to the water – whether in a canoe or rowing boat on the river, or a ferry or sailing yacht out at sea – we leave something of ourselves, as being specifically human, behind us on dry land. Something of our swagger that so often inclines creatures to melt into the landscape or into the vegetation of their habitat at the sight, sound or smell of our arrival. As safe as we may feel with our life jackets, life boats and our modest ability to swim, when we leave the land to peer closer at the world afloat, we in a very basic way take ourselves outside our comfort zone. We entrust ourselves to the safety of our vessel, its stability and impermeability. Moreover, we limit ourselves in our movements to the confines of our boat. Such obvious assumptions, but ones that we would rarely be inclined to consider for very long, if at all. We are not aquatic animals and do not possess wings, and so often we find that those which are and that do seem so very aware, even if only through their own instinct, of the trade-off we have made in our efforts to get closer to them.

It is always an engaging experience, often magical and sometimes even awe inspiring. It is most reaffirming to feel, to however small an extent, the 'otherness' in ourselves and which we look for in the objects of our interest. It is something similar that leads us to seek out the wilderness places and to be swamped by their vastness and relish in our smallness among them. For the great majority of us we will always be the 'other' amidst a world of water. It is just this, no doubt, that can draw the attentions of all, even if only for a few brief moments, to the shores of lake, river, or sea; to bodies of water in all their forms and well before we have any thoughts of leaving the land. The imagination is caught, for all those reasons alluded to above and for the simple fact of its quite obvious differentness to places that we tread everyday. We could be attracted by that seamless definition, via the marshy fringes of some pool or lake that nestles amongst its wooded surrounds or moorland spread, that takes place with both contrast and comfort. Sometimes though, it is that glorious feeling of incongruity as we find with the sea beside the city.

It is perhaps within this latter scenario where the opportunity for experiencing the vastness, even the exhilaration of the wide open coast is of the greatest importance. A sprawl of coastal mud draws the winter birds almost irrespective of the proximity of the built-up environment. If the sea provides there will always be those there to consume. Barely free of the garish delights of the seafront at Southend, I have watched the wading birds in their thousands, endlessly scurrying and stalking the great intertidal sweep of the lower Thames Estuary. Probing the food-rich mud barely beyond the reflected neon glare of the casinos and arcades. Rather further from home and once aboard a ferry on the Bosphorus, crossing from European to Asian Istanbul, I delighted at the Mediterranean Shearwater skimming low across the waves and the Whiskered Terns hung up on the breeze. A deep breath from the clamour and claustrophobia of the city with the minaret skyline only as a backcloth.

Like the wild places, vast also is the untiring swell of the sea. Not only in the meaning of its boundless dimensions and perpetually distant horizons but in the sense of the great energy barely contained within. That which never lets the sea truly rest, always pushing and pulling. Forever drawing into itself and heaving out with unfaltering regularity, but scarcely casting the same shapes, exactly, in the cresting waves, nor throwing the same patterns with the dissipating surf across its surface. With the wind rushing unobstructed across the waves, these are elemental forces that leave us in no doubt as to who or what is in the ascendancy. I am no sailor but find myself at sea on occasion and have often stood and stared from the deck, transfixed by the roll of the waves, steadily pulsating and lifting the steel weight of the boat as if it were merely a leaf raised on gusts of air. Inspired at the idea of coasting across the waves with nothing but the sails bulging invisibly with the wind, yet alarmed at the sight of a wildly flapping sail at the bow and the later knowledge of a sheered metal pin unable to take the strain. Alarmed and impressed, and reminded of my place.

We are truly the 'other' when we take to the sea. It is as such that we may be regarded by some of those that live within it. Some may well have found themselves the object of much scrutiny by inquisitive seals. Animals that seem to have a firm grasp of our abilities in the water, something that the many and various excerpts of wildlife documentary footage has demonstrated, whether we choose to enter the water or remain on deck. Viewing us with that quizzical air that would seem rather more than merely a trait of the animals that we perceive purely in our imagination. In their own way bemused, perhaps, at the lengths we have to go to take to the waves. A few may even have delighted at the sight of dolphins following the slip stream of their boat, leaping from the water with frolicsome regularity and with what would appear to us (and no doubt in reality) as effortless ease. To see such a thing may indeed be the stuff of life ambitions, of a privilege not to be understated. Perhaps with these creatures more than most others, their motives for getting closer to us would go beyond the mere curiosity in the aquatically inept humans at sea on their boat, so numerous are the anecdotes of abiding interaction between each species.

But less unusually and for all of us the gulls sweep through the air with abandon, seeming almost to buff the hulls with their brilliant white and brush the sails with ink-tipped wings. The Cormorants fly past on that low, purposeful course, with those floating within the boat's path diving almost indignantly before surfacing a short distance away. And not only the birds of the sea. I have been out afloat, several kilometres offshore, and encountered a Chaffinch hopping above deck with no obvious hurry to get off and with the same demeanour of a bird in the garden perusing the ground beneath a nut feeder for scraps dropped from above. On the same trip I watched a Kestrel watching me from its perch atop the mainsail, quite unconcerned by the people moving around beneath it. How often would either bird, the falcon in particular, be observed so closely on dry land? It is this indifference, as indeed also are those moments when we find those tables partly turned with ourselves the centre of attention, that we find the opportunity to have a presence among other life without instilling within it a sense of fear.

Seals and dolphins aside however, in other instances, the shifting is more subtle. Fewer might be as quick to think of the becalmed tranquillity of some quiet backwater of an inland river as the scene for a similar exchange, on a rowing boat rather than some sea-going craft. Imagine a river and the small things that when given a moment grow into the consciousness.

The leaning riverside trees, the foliage-laden banks, and the river's contrast to the terrestrial habitats beyond it — things that will always serve to envelop and embrace. All the more so when it offers that unique and delicious atmosphere of inherent coolness wrapping itself around you, offering refreshing relief from a mid-summer sun high in the sky. Within the river, rather than watching from its banks, we can become more a part of it, a somewhat incongruous one when compared to its proper inhabitants, but a part nonetheless.

There is a river that flows quietly through the Essex countryside, a modest river like the many others that flow through many other corners of the country. It is a river that Lola and I discovered for ourselves rather by chance. An afternoon in late spring and we had set our minds on a river walk and sought out one such route on the map. We began our walk but found our views and access to the river consistently frustrated by wide expanses of Stinging Nettles and Bramble barring our way, or screened by trees and thorn bushes. Occasionally, a Banded Demoiselle, that most stunning of damselflies, would wander teasingly from the river and as far as the path, rendering the occasional glimpses of the water all the more frustrating. Our surroundings were pleasant. It was an open, uncluttered landscape. The riparian trees and the spread of bramble and thorn ensured that the air of the ascending spring was never too far away. The wide grassy margins left along the field edges ensured the company of Meadow Brown butterflies as we walked, sharing the bramble blossom with the darker brown Ringlet. But we lacked the closeness of the river that we craved.

We arrived at a road and on crossing it found the footpath to continue past a nursery-cum-garden centre. The path at last ran close to the flowing water, but we now found ourselves cursing the wisdom (presumably of someone connected with the nursery) of planting a dense row of *Leylandii* conifers in between. The nursery, however, soon redeemed itself. The *Leylandii* hedge ended to reveal a full view of the modest but so very inviting river, complete with half a dozen rowing boats nudging the timber boardwalk set against the bank. A few enquiries later and we were afloat, paddling between banks dense with Meadowsweet and Hemp-agrimony, our oars brushing the pads of Yellow Water-lily that floated at the edges. Willow, Alder and Field Maple wove an intermittent tunnel of greenery above our heads which concentrated sparkling colour amid the sunshine that blazed on the water: deep damselfly blues and reds, the softer shades of pale blue Water Forget-me-not on the banks and the delicate pink of Water-plantain at the river's edge. Having endured the starkness of a conifer hedge, shielding the delights of the river just yards away, we now found ourselves utterly and wonderfully removed from the world above and around, absorbed into the world of the river. Absorbed into it and by it.

It is in such instances that, once again, a more intimate view of a place and its wild creatures may be sought. Watching river fish from a small wooden bridge, Wilfred Gavin Brown (*The River*) wrote:

> *"After a time as you are poised above the stream you feel that you are becoming merged in it to a degree that you can never experience if you are only on the bank, and you can feel a greater intimacy with the life that lies amid those waving weeds or in the sombre depths of the mud."*

With the 'life amid the waving weeds', he was no doubt referring mainly to the fish in his stream, but the same may be true for much of the river life. Sit quietly in a boat and the ever-fretful Moorhen might shorten the safe distance that it feels necessary to keep between it and you. The family of Willow Warbler foraging on the abundant insects among the

Alder branches above scarcely respond to your presence. Perhaps even the Water Vole might be more content to continue its munching of the stems in clearer view by the bank. Damselflies settle on the boat, with gleaming eyes and vivid colour, even trying to alight on the oars as you row near to the water's edge, whilst their shining splendour flashes closer into view, enough to hear the flutter of wings as they pass over your shoulder. The river knows that you are out of sorts on the water and teems with unperturbed intent. The life of the river closes around you all the more tightly when it hardly notices you are there.

Maybe it is not a 'peculiar' thing at all that happens when we take to the water. Different perhaps, but only peculiar in the unfamiliarity of our experience. It offers us a chance to engage more harmoniously with our surroundings and the beings that inhabit it; an opportunity to be more *of* our environment as well as simply being in it. This is in truth, and at risk of undermining the whole ethos of this chapter, something that may be achieved anywhere, with a small effort of observation and patience. Sit quietly for long enough beneath the shade of a tree in a corner of a meadow and soon enough you find yourself drawn into and accepted as a small part of the landscape. Assume a passive presence on the edge of some forest clearing and before long there will be tits twittering above your head and the company of the wild mammals of the wood become a genuine possibility. At the very least by way of its smaller inhabitants, the mass of life that fills such a place will begin to reveal itself in all its multiplicity.

But on water it *is* different. We *are* different. Our own outlook has altered before we begin to consider how the attitude of the wild creatures may change around us. An account by Edward A. Armstrong, *Birds of the Grey Wind*, not of being on the water but of photographing Rooks from a hide constructed high up in a tree, nevertheless has a familiarity to it. Similarly outside his regular circumstances, even as a keen ornithologist and no stranger to the inside of a bird hide, he observed that *"The earth seems very far away and the elevation gives a sense of aloofness… A keener edge is on all one's perceptions."* Perhaps taken outside our normal context, our own senses do become more alert to the life around us (something which in certain circumstances would constitute a most useful survival instinct). Consciously or subconsciously, we can take less for granted of our situation and surroundings. Amid the world afloat we can only and unavoidably take a different perspective, one which might give that keener edge and a clearer reflection on both ourselves and our natural environment.

Middle Ground?

Where is the centre of a place? Is the centre the same as the middle? The latter maybe refers to the *actual* point that is as equidistant from the edges as it can be, the irregularities of shape not withstanding. If so, then what of the centre? This is all very much a matter of some subjectivity. If it makes more sense to make the 'centre' the 'middle' and the 'middle' the 'centre', then please reverse them as you see fit. But to my mind it is the middle that should refer to the actual, physical middle of a place and the centre that should be imbued with rather more laterally contrived and subjective ideas. This is all a rather frivolous, even pedantic consideration of definition and perspective, but an intriguing one to pursue nonetheless.

The centre need not be defined in purely physical terms. Sure enough, it is a point within a place, but a point that to another would appear as quite randomly chosen. To whoever defined it as such, it is anything but. It is the position on an axis around which a whole place can revolve. It is a most significant point on a curve of a graph that depicts the living of life in a place. The centre is a point of focus more than of measurement. A single small pool, half hidden by reeds and which by dint of some aspect of it that grasped the imagination and sense of fascination, could be that around which a mosaic of marshy fields and thick, scrubby hedgerows are centred. Or even a wider area than that. The places on a map of an area that you are especially connected with, or have lived and grown up. The centre is a place in mind as much, or perhaps more so, as a place on the ground. The centre of a wood could be the grandest oak tree that stands like an imperious among the others around. Or a most idyllic, flower-filled glade, gleaming with sunlight that breaks the canopy shading the ground beyond it. It could be things like these, but it doesn't have to be. The centre of a range of mountains need not be the highest summit but rather a lesser place (in terms of magnitude), connected more with feelings than purely physical qualities.

A wood near where I live, which I have known throughout my life, has many notable trees and interesting features, just as you would expect from any fine, ancient wood. It has centuries-old oaks and tall, graceful birch trees. It has peaceful stretches of quietly murmuring brook, whose sunlit waters reflect on the smooth trunks of the Hornbeam that stand on its banks. It is a place full of memories going back many years: of seeing Purple Hairstreak butterflies for the first time flicking around the crown of a prominent oak, or a local rarity, a Wood Warbler, that stopped by early one autumn, or watching Spotted Flycatchers nesting in the bough of an oak tree at the crossing of two rides. Three of a great many. All things that could serve to provide the wood with its centre point and which indeed occupy a prominent position in my collective experience of the place. Yet it was not these that prompted this particular shifting of perspective.

It was in fact a Crab Apple tree that I have passed by many times. A tree you would scarcely notice during the bareness of winter, when perhaps the only colour is borrowed from the Jays that pause from their seasonal foraging among its branches, or the twittering tit flocks examining the tree with similar intentions. In the summer its foliage melds, as a squat and rather untidy pillar of green, with the oaks that stand above and the Hornbeam that grow nearby. With its blossom-heavy branches, it is in the spring that it is undoubtedly at its most remarkable. I had noticed it before, of course, admired it and appreciated its presence in a wood in which the native apple is not exactly a prolific tree. But only now had it registered with a more singular significance, more specifically within the context of its surroundings.

A blossom-laden Crab Apple is a thing of beauty in itself. This one was full of white petals, so plentiful as to dominate the greenery of the leaves underneath. But rather than simply pause by it as I walked past, to allow my eyes to do justice to the fine display of flower, I found myself almost transfixed by it. For an hour I circled the tree, peering into and around the blooms and among the branches (and doubtlessly appearing somewhat eccentric to passers-by). I had my camera and started snapping a visual record of some of the many insects also drawn to the dazzling white flare of flowers, drawn to this abundance of nectar whilst – being mid-April – many of the other woodland flowers were still awakening. The tree was simply twitching to the buzz of wings and the guzzling of proboscises. The Blackcap that had been singing from within it did not stay long with my approach but soon after stopping a Green-veined White butterfly took leave from the warm spring sunshine to drink for a few moments from the blossom. No fewer than eight species of bee were directing their attentions towards the tree. Toiling about the flowers were queen Common Carder Bee and the first of the new generation of Early-nesting Bumblebee workers that I had seen that spring. There were at least a couple of different species of mining bee, solitary bees that nest communally in burrows in the soil. And also the Nomad bees that parasitize the mining bee nests, although while nectaring alongside their would-be hosts, any more sinister connotations were left in the ground. Droneflies and other hoverflies zipped around the tree, whilst a bumblebee-mimicking Bee-fly probed the flowers with a long, needle-thin proboscis.

Although not realising it until taking my thoughts back home with me, I had found the centre of the wood, or rather *my* centre of the wood. It didn't seem likely at the time that any other given area of the wood could have such a level of activity and variety of life than this one. It really did feel like a hub, a kind of epicentre of a place where the spring is gathering momentum and is preparing for the imminent explosion of fervent productivity that makes the season the joy that it is. I gained a sense, perhaps rather in my own imagination, of the life of the wood radiating from this point. This, it has to be said, would necessitate a somewhat simplistic view of woodland life. In reality it is a mesh, woven copiously from the myriad threads of the myriad lives within it. But maybe at that moment, during that period of such abundant flowering, there was some truth in my romantic positioning of the tree within the wood.

What trails, I wondered, would be drawn if one could gain an aerial view and trace the paths of all those creatures that were lured there. The flitting butterflies in search of the sun and the females searching for host plants on which to lay their eggs wandered where the spring breeze and the distribution of their food plants took them. The mining bees that would have made their excavations elsewhere, into some sunny, south-facing bank, perhaps along the brook. The Honeybees that could well have been commuting between the tree and their hive in a garden many tens, perhaps even hundreds of metres away. And the bumblebees – the workers delivering their foraged pollen back to their nests; and the queens with their zigzag scouring, so intently over the ground for likely places to found their own colonies. What topographies must the bumblebee see in the landscape imperceptible to us? Isn't one old mouse hole more or less the same as the next? Just as one patch of likely looking grassy vegetation over here is pretty much like the other one over there. Yet time after time potential sites are rejected by a queen on her apparent quest to scrutinise every square centimetre of ground available before making a choice. It once again becomes evident that we just don't see as much of the world as we think we do. And yes, considering all of this, I had not only discovered a centre in the mind but had also, at least to some small extent, located one in reality.

A month later and the apple cast a different presence. Unusually warm spring weather had brought the wood early into flush. Not just Hornbeam and birch which break buds early in the spring but oaks were also already in full leaf. The now flowerless apple had been absorbed into the wood by means of one of the oak trees above it with whose branches it mingled. But, for me, the presence that it had assumed weeks before remained. Greenery among green, it continued to feel like the centre of the wood, even without the ascending buzz of early spring resurgence. I knew that the tree still heaved with life, but also that to see it I would have to look harder.

The only butterflies around were — outstandingly — the few Heath Fritillary butterflies that fluttered past me and along the brightly sun-lit ride. These insects are a great rarity in British woodlands and as good a reason as any to be revisiting my apple tree. The Carder Bees were understandably more interested in the emerging yellow trumpets of the Common Cow-wheat growing beside the path than the developing fruits on the branches. So too the fritillaries, as the cow-wheat is their food plant. But the tree was still full of life, life though that endeavoured for the most part to remain unseen. I have no doubt that it was present in the same quantities as before and that I managed to observe only a small proportion of it, but enough to gain a sense of its plenty.

Now effectively mostly out of sight, the crab apple still had its creatures that wove, or would come to weave, their paths throughout the wood, just as it had with those of the early spring. Some perhaps would not reach as far as the bumblebees and others I watched back then, but reach they would all the same. The one superbly camouflaged Oak Bush-cricket nymph that I located was presumably not alone from its kind within the apple. They are the most arboreal of the UK Orthoptera (grasshoppers, crickets, etc.) and in spite of their name are not particularly associated with oak but a whole range of deciduous trees and shrubs. This small, translucent green insect was barely a third of the length of the adult it would grow into. There was a group of 28 moth eggs (I am fairly sure there are no apple-feeding butterflies in this wood) placed with obvious and meticulous care on the underside of a leaf, one batch of surely many others and of different species. The apple is known to support a huge range of Lepidopteran life. More than 70 species in fact. Included among these are the Short-cloaked Moth and Clouded Silver that I know have been recorded in this wood. Elsewhere, a caterpillar had fashioned a curious looking cylindrical cocoon, just a few millimetres in length, standing upright on the upperside of a leaf. It was made by one of the *Coleophora* species, possibly the Apple and Plum Case-bearer moth, tiny micro-moths whose caterpillars devour the inside of the leaf to leave blotches or galleries where they have fed within the intact remaining leaf. I had noticed at least two different kinds of leaf-mine before encountering this chrysalis.

Whilst not being able to identify all of them to species, I noted as many as I had seen a month previously. Another leaf was caked with grey-coloured aphids, newly hatched from overwintering eggs and yet to disperse from their place of shelter. I shook a few branches over my note book to reveal the presence of several species of spider, plus tiny black weevils and numerous minuscule flies. Little wonder then that I should also notice the black and red Sailor Beetle lurking amid the foliage, a predator of small invertebrates.

I made a third visit a few weeks later, with summer fast approaching. The life of the tree seemed even more hidden than before. But many creatures had been at work in my absence. Some of the leaves were marked by other leaf-miners, this time leaving long, sinuous trails within the leaf, rather than the blotches I had seen before. Many more were variously chomped, nibbled or stripped to a lattice by numerous jaws and probing mouthparts. I could assume that some of the feasters were still within the tree by the attentions of the predators and parasitoids scrutinising the branches; ichneumon wasps, females with long needle-like ovipositors, searching for caterpillars to inject their eggs into and hence later recipients of their own all devouring larvae, and empid flies lurking on the lookout for other sunbathing flies on which to pounce. Maybe also the Blackcap that I heard singing back at the beginning of spring had returned on occasion to take his fill. And following the Honeysuckle bines infiltrating and threading around the branches, back down to their points of issue from the ground, my attention was drawn by the still immature Meadow Grasshopper and numerous Dark Bush-crickets sunning themselves on the lower leaves at the foot of the tree. Imagining also the moths of the night-time wood supping from those sweetest of sweet smelling blooms, I was given another reminder of the strands of life that emanate and interweave from any one point within a wider area.

To see the tree in late summer was to experience the mood of a whole season given focus to a single organism. The branches were heavy with fruit. Caterpillars were fat. Flies buzzed lazily around the branches, hardly bothering to retreat more than a few twig lengths away, should my approach disturb them from their 'hoovering' of the leaf surfaces for some invisible attractant. Perhaps it was the honeydew they were after, excreted by the abundant aphids that fell onto my notebook when I shook the branches. Aphids and the little yellow insects that I supposed to be the closely related Apple Psyllid, *Psyla mali*. The ladybirds that crawled among the foliage would surely have rich pickings.

It was a warm and slightly humid late-August afternoon. Few things among the wood revealed their presence as I walked through it, just as was mirrored by the life hidden among the apple, but which rained down so plentifully onto the open pages. Life everywhere was unhurried but intent, unseen but ever-present. It was almost as if the whole place was encumbered by the accumulated sum of its own fecundity. The fruit on the branches prompted thoughts of unflustered, but assured preparation. Of readiness for a change to come that would barely be perceived by those that moved among the comfortable weight of the summer air. If a plant could behave lazily then this tree had achieved it.

This is how a place finds its centre. The middle is fixed, but the centre changes from observer to observer. Maybe also it is something that could change with season or mood. The dragonflies that dash over the sun-sparkled summer pool will later fade into autumn, just as elsewhere a view is filled by the changing leaves that set a scene ablaze with colour. And as the leaves are lost to the drawing of winter, then it is towards the avian hustle of a frosted marsh and the ice-encrusted heads of the gathered reeds that the centre might shift.

In this instance though, it was very much located in the one place, static amidst the flux of the spring that washed around it towards the flood of summer. A kind of rock held fast amid the constantly changing currents of life around it. It is now somewhere that will be fixed throughout the seasons. Not only in the fervent flush of spring and the overflowing of summer but also with its spreading tints of autumn colour and fallen fruit and its attentive scavengers. A time when only a handful of creatures still seek shelter among the lessening foliage: the little green leafhoppers that remain active well into the autumn, the tiny black flea beetles that spring away as soon as they are discovered, or the few psyllids and aphids that hang on into the earlier weeks of the autumn. In the winter its centre may exist more firmly within the imagination than at other times, but each Magpie that pauses in its branches, each Great Spotted Woodpecker that alights to search among the crevices of its bark, will register and be noted. And no doubt, even then, some passing gang of Long-tailed Tits will pause and find some invertebrate morsel or other among the cold, bare bark. This offers up a pleasing contradiction in that how can we have a fixed point amid this landscape of change, which itself has engaged the onlooker through its own cycles of change and those of the organisms around and among it?

Rather less frivolous and pedantic as these musings started out, does all this also give us an inkling of how we might find our own place within things? If the idea of the centre point is a subjective one, then that point resides individually within us, which in some small way we may use in an attempt to orientate ourselves within the intricacies of life. If not, then at the very least it provides us with the vantage point from which we can experience the stunning complexity of the natural world in its finer detail.

Part 3

Common Ground

Common Ground

> *"...Little we see in Nature that is ours;*
> *We have given our hearts away, a sordid boon!*
> *The Sea that bares her bosom to the moon;*
> *The winds that will be howling at all hours,*
> *And are up-gathered now like sleeping flowers;*
> *For this and everything, we are out of tune..."*

William Wordsworth (1770-1850), from *Out of Tune*

There is often talk of our common ground with the rest of nature, of 'being at one with nature', to quote the well-known phrase. It is something that we all feel, everyone of us, even if it is just an inkling. Who could not afford themselves just a brief moment to look out across the sea and realise for a second that fleeting contemplation of its vastness, even if swamped by the most clamorous din of some busy seaside resort? And there must be few who would walk past a pond without feeling a slight twang of curiosity for what might be rippling its surface or even perhaps for what lurks underneath? Yes, these might be just inklings, but ones which all the same sit at one end of the sliding scale that includes engrossment, fascination, awe and wonder. The same, it should also be said, where we may also experience connection with our fellow species. This then is surely the start of our consideration of what 'being at one with nature' is all about.

In seeking to achieve this common ground is to remind ourselves of the core ideas of renewing and reinforcing a view of the natural world beyond our more casual, but nonetheless meaningful, initial impressions. This is something that is not actually necessary in order for us to appreciate the things in our natural surroundings, but to understand their importance may be as enlightening as it is rewarding. The inevitable irony in re-looking at how we connect with things – at our place within it all – is that any resultant shift of perspective might facilitate a simpler relationship with nature than previously experienced, through making our engagement with it more easily achieved and perhaps returning some of its sense of honesty back into our lives. There is always a danger here to be overwhelmed by the misty haze of romanticism for bygone days of 'honest' living when all were closely attuned to the seasonal rhythms and when our own hearts beat in time with the land, and for us to forget just how tough life must have been in such times; nature can be as brutal at it is beautiful. There is, though, something to be gained from this wistful nostalgia. Some of that honesty does seem genuine and relevant, and is worth searching for and assimilating back into our own modern day life and lifestyles.

That we lack, as a culture, so much of this connectivity is of detriment to us on various levels: biologically, culturally, and to each of us as individuals. But why? What is the nature of these ties that makes them so relevant and even so fundamental to the human condition? This is a question not easily answered and a vast area for study in itself. I trust you will forgive me if it is not necessarily done full justice here. Nevertheless, the idea that it is not a connection with nature that we might look to gain but rather the reconnection to that which is forgotten to all but our most instinctive selves surely presents a significant starting point.

The notion of our separateness from nature is a most curious one. It is one borne from the messages of our culture. We might be given to believe that we are indeed separate from the natural world and that it exists chiefly for our exploitation and benefit. This is, one could argue, exacerbated and most relevantly in the case of the developed world, by the ever-increasing role of technology in our lives that, admittedly with a great generalisation on the benefits and otherwise of modern innovation, might further affirm that illusion of separateness. The technological world (and don't get me wrong, I am not attempting to take a moral high ground on this one – since – I am typing the text on a laptop and not a typewriter!) in so many cases does not exactly encourage us towards the most tactile pleasures of the world around us. Rather, it gives us so many more reasons and excuses to stay indoors and to not actually experience things at the most primary of levels. Sure enough, humankind has taken too many steps along the path of 'progress' for them all to be retraced. Few of us in the Western world could or would want to live like the so-called 'noble savage', but does that necessarily mean that we have lost our place in the natural order of things? We couldn't even if we tried, although by increasing our distance from it we heighten that sense of alienation with the world and also perhaps with a part of ourselves. The consequences of this appear to be unfolding day by day.

Any ideas of separateness are folly. We have so much in common with the rest of nature, so how could they be otherwise? Yes, we do have those things that make us distinctly human; we have art, literature, music and love. There are obviously a great many ways in which we are not like other animals, but by the same token there are many ways in which they are not like us. Yet all things still need to achieve the same goals in their lives, albeit in differing levels of ritual and complexity: to find sustenance and shelter, to breathe and breed. It is the same biosphere in which each organism must acquire its resources necessary for life. None of this represents any kind of philosophical revelation, nor is it intended to, but it is necessary when considering the idea of common ground.

Obviously, outside of such biological necessity our power of intellect, at least in one respect, does set us well apart from most, if not all other life. It may be this along with the cynicisms of the modern world that ironically provides one of the greatest obstacles between us and the sense of belonging that lingers at the edge of our thoughts. The encumbrance of age and experience on the imagination of our childhood that once allowed us to engage so completely and unconditionally with our interactions with the world. The young mind, unaware of itself, is capable of grasping the fullness of time, the *eternity* – in a manner of speaking – of the moment. The child places the whole of its existence into the *now* and relishes, without knowing, in its endless possibilities, its unchanging but boundless potential. It sees a world full of objects – the people that occupy the world and anything else that exists within its sphere of experience. Objects that merely oscillate within the flow of passing days and not assuming that linear course that ultimately all things, not least time itself, must follow. The child greets the days without the encumbrances of expectation and all the uncertainties that come to accompany it. Where real experience of the world is wanting, the imagination fills in the gaps.

We grow, we learn and we come to know the truer value of things. But the gaps still remain and we miss the child within us. From this springs nostalgia, those fond thoughts that we might dare not delve too deeply for risk of tainting them with the truisms of life that adulthood has exposed us to. But shouldn't we take full account of these warm childhood memories but without disregarding the learned experiences that come after? Can the nostalgia not provide the reference points around which to orientate the gathered wisdom (such as that may be) of the experiences of life? This is surely so, given the way that we all learn from our mistakes and accumulate our life experience from our erroneous actions and subsequent reflection, but in view of those 'gaps that remain' – those nagging omissions in our sense of the fullness of things – so often 'never the twain shall meet'.

The past can drag a heavy weight on the mind, while thoughts of the future flit erratically on the edge of the rational, like a half-glimpsed movement over water: the play of the sun among the river's ripple, or the flash of the same across some pearlescent wing, lost into the glare of the light? To release the inertia and lay eyes on those glanced impressions of what lies ahead, is to fix the moment, just as the child unwittingly does, even if only fleetingly; to defy, as best we can, the moment's unfaltering inexorability. It is each moment in relation to the others that go before and ahead of it that gives it the *substance* of experience and the illusion of stasis. In the older mind it is this that requires an imaginative effort, yet in the young it seems something as instinctive as breathing.

The illusion is just that. It serves, though, to capture for long enough those moments so that they are felt. Not that we become aware of each one as it passes, constantly in observation of that linear passage of time – the thought of it would be demoralising beyond words – and anyway it would not provide any real, tangible experience. Rather, each is filled and not merely spent. What we are left with in fact is a kind of net product, so subtle as to leave us with a profound sense of place, of spaces being filled. That one might even think to ponder these possibilities as done here, gives ample indication of the drain of the imaginative self that takes place when we leave the realms of childhood. Innocence is key and is lost as soon as we understand what it is (the same can be said of ignorance, as we cannot truly be ignorant if we know what we are supposed to be ignorant about; if we continue to behave as such then we are less ignorant than unreasonable). It is not realistic to suppose that we could live our lives in such a consciously philosophical way; to do so misses the point of re-emphasising and enjoying our experience of our natural environment. Yet to raise an awareness that we are intermittently conscious of promotes a freer, if not necessarily clearer, perspective on things.

The child is immersed in this state of being, this most natural condition, perhaps that of nature itself. Maybe it was something of this that the famous Swiss psychologist Carl

Gustav Jung was alluding to when he recalled (as quoted by E.L. Grant Watson in *The Mystery of Physical Life*): *"From a low hill in the Athi plains of East Africa I once watched the vast herds of wild animals grazing in soundless stillness as they had done from time immemorial, touched only by the breath of a primeval world."* He continues to explain: *"I felt then as if I were the first man, the first creature to know that all this **is**. The entire world around me was in its primeval state; it did not know that it **was**."* Just as the child accepts each day without question of its implications or a comprehensive sense of its transitory 'existence', so too does the impassivity of nature imply that it also is concerned only with being, without the yearning for knowing beyond the externalities of its physical parts. Still on the Athi plains, Jung goes on to make the rather lofty claim on the part of the human race that: *"…without that moment it would never have been. All Nature seeks this goal and finds it fulfilled in man."* To assume that we are the *raison d'être* of all nature is a matter of further discussion, but it does appear very likely that it only truly finds the faculty of introspection and objectivity via the thoughts of humankind.

Debating such questions is almost something of an aside in the context considered here. The very idea of us providing some kind of pinnacle to the intellectual potentialities of nature unavoidably sets us firmly within it; we become both the observer and the observed. Jung mentioned that 'moment' in which he contemplated that his presence amid primeval life allowed nature to somehow know itself. The point at which the moment experienced by the observer connects with each simultaneous moment experienced, however dully or indeed even metaphorically, by each living thing and each of the processes and interactions of the life taking place around him.

With this considered, we once again entertain the idea of a connectivity with other life – with all life – in a most fundamental sense, perhaps even across time as well as the space occupied by *our* biosphere. A physicist I most certainly am not, and this is a tangent that I will not, or indeed could not, pursue further. It does, nevertheless, fix more firmly in the mind that 'folly of separateness'.

But the question might still remain: how much do we all have in common with the multitudinous other, so obviously different organisms with which we share our planet? How intrinsic are the ties that bind all of life inextricably together? Conjecture on the subject seems to reside in the murky realms of postulation and the subjectivity of 'gut-feeling' (as I have no doubt ably demonstrated!). There have been scientists, writers and thinkers, and some of not inconsiderable eminence, that would postulate that such ties have their origins beyond even the principles of the ecological functioning of the Earth, something further than the inevitable interrelationships of species and their environments. E. L. Grant Watson (1885-1970), previously mentioned, was a zoologist and writer during the early to mid-20th century. In 1964 he published *The Mystery of Physical Life*, a book of substantial depth (often perplexingly so) in consideration of the fundamental characteristics and qualities of the dazzling variety of life on our planet. In the book he presented and developed the idea *"that the Darwinian theory of evolution through chance variations and natural selection is too simple to meet the complicated and evasive patterns that Nature presents."* It is an assertion that perhaps should not be too hastily disregarded, even by the staunchest Darwinist. He clearly had strong thoughts towards a holistic view of life on our planet, positioning the human race firmly within the midst of it all. He wrote of the possibility of *"making our subjective feeling an object of our scrutiny"* and in doing so *"enter into relation with creatures of our observation."* He even referred to Jung's theories described in *Archetypes and the Collective Unconscious*, in which the author argues the presence of some element of instinct in our own subconscious mind, present throughout nature, thus allowing for the possibility of the connectivity of things beyond the physicality of life.

This would seem to some, myself included, to be rather radical, somewhat pseudo-religious-pantheism. It does, though, throw up the potential for interesting alternatives for how we see our relationship with the rest of nature. Not necessarily by accepting what certainly seems a somewhat uncomfortable leap of reasoning, but to consider not only the connections between things but perhaps also the nature, or the significance, of those interactions. Watson's was an imaginative stance – one perhaps that again might require we rediscover those lost faculties of our younger days. The whole of an oak tree is far greater than the sum of its parts, as is the sense of contentment we might experience when we see and enjoy and relish its presence. It is more than can be measured in an empirical sense. As Watson himself engagingly puts it: *"only the properties of nature can be described in quantitative terms. We can weigh a mouse, and know the length of its ears and tail, but we cannot measure the quality of mousehood."*

The idea of experiencing the connectedness of things is not such a far-fetched one. There are many, I dare to suggest, that have experienced that sense of connection with nature, here alluded to a sense of engagement beyond simply observing in the more literal context with our eyes. Something that might be gained through experiencing a sense of belonging with a place and the contentedness that comes with it. It might arise through a more fine-tuned feeling of empathy within our surroundings and the organisms that occupy it. Not in a literal sense of feeling what a beetle feels and understanding the concept of being a tree rooted to the earth (although the poet Edward Thomas (1878-1917) does in his poem *Aspens* in *Edward Thomas Selected Poems*), but in the admittedly more vague notion of a level of appreciation of the chaotic order and purposefulness that prevails in the primeval essence of nature.

Think once more of a river, winding through its upland reaches and its waters frothing against the huge stones that tumble down to rest on the riverbed for centuries, maybe millennia. Think of the repetition of the water lapping against the smoothed boulders, but with each impact of water on stone never truly the same as any before. Think of the moss that clothes the moistened rock and the damp earth, and which smothers the buttressed roots straining to brace the trees that lean and tower over the torrent below them. Think of the depths that flicker in and out of the grasp of your eyesight, leaving more to your imagination than your gaze. And the small beings that are scarcely observed: the water nymphs that draw in the Dippers and draw up the trout. Think of the night river and the imagined beings: the Otter upstream, the flight of bats consumed by the darkness, the looming canopy above and the ceaseless sounds of water on stone and on earth, gulping and swirling and filling the blackness and drawing you deeper within it.

Light or dark, the action of the water captivates, ever-changing, ever restless. We follow the flow or rest our gaze on the chaotic rhythms on a certain place of its passing. For those moments the river holds our senses; the dance of the surface fixes our eyes, the din of a billion points of conflict envelops; the coolness on the skin, the smell of wet earth, the sweet air. Each glide of the Golden-ringed Dragonfly, each poignant ascent of the Mayfly, each flick of the Wagtail's yellow flash all weave a thread and tighten the mesh.

Trying to attune yourself to the patterns and rhythms, even, dare I say, to the instinctiveness of your surroundings, everything lifts itself into your consciousness and everything brings the same significance to the scene, whether the fluttering caddis flies and tiny winged insects that chance the wash or the massive oaks and elegant alders that rise from the banks. You are keenly aware of each detail, yet simultaneously enveloped by the entirety of your environs. I suspect that it was just this kind of experience one *"star-lit evening"* of which Richard Jefferies wrote: *"I was sensitive to all things; to the least blade of grass, to the largest oak. They seemed like exterior nerves and veins for the conveyance of feeling to me.*" Each thing, each aspect of the scene, although raised towards your awareness, as individual components paradoxically lose a part of their meaning and it is instead the crossing of paths, the interactions, the connections among each of them, living or elemental, that become more significant. Each interaction, each blurring of boundaries, each connection adds that much to the whole. On much firmer, scientific ground, Edward O. Wilson firmly rejects the Jungian idea that "*some remnant of psychological continuity exists across that immense phylogenetic* [i.e. the history of evolutionary development] *gulf*", but even he speaks of "*some general order within the exciting chaos, some powerful process to be uncovered.*" The same which I think Wilson was aware of, but this time encompassing that other process of natural selection.

Within this more scientific context, the idea of the holism of nature has perhaps best (and at first controversially) been elucidated by James Lovelock's Gaia Hypothesis (see Lovelock, 1979) and subsequent theory put forward initially in the late 1970s and named after the Greek goddess of the Earth. Since life appeared on the Earth the sun has apparently increased its energy output by as much as 30%. In pondering why the Earth's temperature should have remained pretty much constant in spite of this, Lovelock proposed in his book *Gaia: A new Look at Life on Earth*:

> "*...that the physical, and chemical composition for the Earth, of the atmosphere and of the oceans has been and is actively made fit and comfortable by the presence of life itself. This is in contrast to the conventional wisdom which held that life adapted to planetary conditions as it and they evolved their separate ways.*"

By way of setting the scene, an example (presented, I should add, in the simplest of terms – the pages of this book and the author of its words would not do the subject any justice at all!) being the potentially important role of wetland microbes that produce millions of tonnes of methane each year. Through chemical reaction and the bonding of methane molecules with those of excess oxygen, the quantity of oxygen in the atmosphere can be regulated to the optimum 21% and prevent a gradual accumulation, with other processes ensuring the continued input of sufficient levels of the gas; too little and life would not be able to flourish, too much and with more oxygen to fuel them the likelihood of uncontrollable raging forest fires would increase and ravage the ecosystems of the Earth.

His hypothesis proved to be controversial and was lambasted by much of the scientific establishment at the time (which, as a staunchly independent scientist and multi-disciplinary *"general practitioner"*, Lovelock was eventually happy to be apart from) with such eminent scientific thinkers as Richard Dawkins stating, and not without good reason, that *"there was no way for evolution by natural selection to lead to altruism on a global scale."*

With the benefit of a subsequent 30 or so years' of experience and scientific development, such vehement opposition might seem rather surprising. Indeed, many of James Lovelock's ideas, theories and predictions have come to provide the basis for more recent scientific research. It is not difficult, for this author's humble ponderings at any rate, to think of the Earth and its life forms as indeed a single interrelated system. There is an intuitiveness to the idea, given what we know, for example, about the influence that the great tropical forests have on the global climate or how the ecological relations between a predator and its prey maintain a cycle of apparently stable dynamism through the cyclical effects on one and other by their constantly rising and falling populations. There seems no obvious reason why an evolving process of natural selection and this holistic notion of the planet should not exist in unison. Natural selection requires that environmental pressures favour certain characteristics in individuals within a population, which are in turn maintained over generations, but why shouldn't the process be a two-way affair, with organisms influencing environment (by way of mere causes and effects and not through any altruistic motivations) and environment influencing organisms in a state of steady flux? I may be oversimplifying the scenario, but that intuitive sense of it remains strong in my mind providing the most fundamental platform for the common ground of life on our planet.

The idea of altruism on the part of life on Earth was indeed a significant sticking point for Gaia. It has to be said that the tone of the initial 1979 book – *Gaia: A new look at life on Earth* – did, at times, rather reflect the words of criticism it received. Even though Lovelock maintained that "*nowhere in our writings do we express the idea that planetary self-regulation is purposeful, or involves foresight of planning by the biota*", it was criticism, however, that was taken on board, even met with gratitude and used to strengthen the reasoning behind Gaia. He later revised his hypothesis, accepting the flaws in the original and stating: "*I now think that regulation, at a state fit for life, is the property of the whole evolving system of life, air, ocean and rocks.*" He wrote again about Gaia in 2000 in *The Ages of Gaia*, developing his theories and presenting the evidence for the so-called geophysical view of the Earth as Gaia.

Even prior to this, the 1979 book provided a most compelling argument and description of the processes by which conditions are sustained by the life present within their influence. Indeed, Lovelock never originally denied the evolutionary process. The only error of judgement perhaps, as he later admitted himself, was to view the evolution of species as being, to a certain extent, separate from the development of 'Gaia'. Perhaps his lamentations for the 'closed-shop' attitudes of the individual scientific disciplines still echo something of these more radical origins of Gaia, reminding us, for instance, of his take on the geologists' view that "*the Earth is just a ball of rock, moistened by the oceans; that nothing but a tenuous film of air excludes the hard vacuum of space; and that life is merely an accident, a quiet passenger that happens to have hitched a ride.*" Need we have a problem with uniting such a view as this with the idea that everything living and non-living within the Earth's biosphere is interlinked and interactive? That life on Earth is an 'accident' and an overwhelmingly unlikely one at that serves only to enhance our wonder and deeply felt fascinations. . And for whatever reason, these rocks, oceans and atmosphere, and the life that exists within and on them, has undoubtedly allowed something very remarkable to take places over the aeons.

Whether one is to accept the notion of Lovelock's Gaia or otherwise, the interconnectedness of life even when viewed from much more of a lay-person's perspective is difficult to ignore. Watson's "*evasive patterns*", Wilson's "*exciting chaos*" and Lovelock's 'Gaia' each allude to the same idea. Everything has its place, its causes and effects. Ecologists have their 'keystone species', around which the integrity of natural communities might, to an extent, pivot. A classic illustration of this (familiar to a great many ecology students, past and present) is the theoretical removal of the wolf from its theoretical food web. No top predator and there is nothing to keep the deer population or other herbivores in check. More deer results in increased levels of browsing and grazing. This has an impact on the ground flora, resulting in the loss of species. Less floral diversity equals less invertebrate diversity which in turn has ramifications for the vertebrates and invertebrates that feed in and on them. What do the wolf and deer, plants and insects of a remote ecosystem have to do with us and our acquisition of resources and such like? It doesn't take too much to appreciate how on a larger scale the gradual chipping away on the building blocks of the world's ecosystems can and does lead to more directly deleterious consequences for humanity.

The trickle of disturbance caused by, say, a species of butterfly going extinct might not have a direct or perceptibly noticeable effect on anything but those most immediately associated with it, like a species of plant particularly adapted to being pollinated by the butterfly or some other animal that depends on the caterpillars to complete its own life cycle. But then the trickles of disturbance created by the demise of these other 'dependants' broaden the influence of our extinct butterfly more widely to the other beings that depend on them. With enough extinctions and enough barely perceptibly trickles braiding outwards, they can meet with others and combine their influence into a stronger flow, and so on and so forth. From trickles to a stream and from streams into rivers; how much longer for the deluge to build?

Lovelock's regulation mechanisms often revolved around the life processes of microbial organisms that have *en masse* crucial consequences for the chemical components of the air and oceans. These are elements, of course, on which all of the larger plants and animals depend and on which they in turn bring their own influences to bear – the cycles of energy and chemicals – the stuff of life – passing through all organisms (ourselves included), quite irrespective of size, stature or their perceived position within the scheme things; once again we might bring to mind thoughts of reconnection rather than connection.

Those philosophical leanings with which this chapter began may have arrived at a more empirical standpoint or at least one which prompts thoughts rather more towards the tangibilities of the potential relationships of life on our planet. Whatever, our assumption should be the same – we should view nothing in isolation. In some ways the very idea of seeking 'common ground' with the rest of nature is a nonsense if one is to accept this deeply intrinsic view of life on Earth for which there seems ample reason to. Perhaps though, this is a measure of just how far removed from nature we have become, but how significant our bonds nevertheless are to it.

Human Needs

In the light of the considerations of the previous chapter, the question might reasonably be raised as to the need to delve so deeply. Whether we should merely accept as being good without further unnecessary dissection, something of which we are perhaps only vaguely aware? But then human nature will always lead us to pursuing our paths of contemplation as far as we need or are able to take them. And it might also be argued that such reaffirmation of our place in the world – in the natural world – will be of great benefit to us on a number of different levels and not only in such ways as has just been considered. In the light of a less intrinsic view of ourselves within nature, the idea of 'human needs' might in some ways seem contradictory to these thoughts of 'common ground', but it is within the latter that the former is firmly rooted.

Even if the context of our alignment with nature at its most fundamental is rather difficult to pin down, wouldn't its significance in relation to each of us, individually and culturally, be easier to identify? Needless to say, the importance of the natural environment in this context, away from the more easily perceived quantitative values of hard cash and fiscal gain, has proved notoriously difficult to define, hence its alarming and continued degradation. What 'value' are oceans that cannot be fished, forests whose timber cannot be extracted, or land that cannot be farmed or developed? The future of the conservation and preservation of the world's natural heritage has an increasingly realised need for including the fishermen, foresters and farmers within the equation through sensitive and sustainable operations. But taking them on face value for now, we instinctively know that these things have value in such a context, even aside from those utilitarian benefits, but how to articulate them is another matter entirely, a major contributing factor to the past – and unfortunately ongoing –

short-term and wholly unsustainable exploitation of our natural resources.

Such contemplation is to somewhat move away from the intended prompting of thought, but it would seem crass to talk of the human needs and values of nature without putting them in the albeit rather grim context of the state of our planet as I write. Indeed, in this context the benefits of nature to humans are all too obvious and the crumbling integrity of our natural heritage all the more painful for it. Aside from any cultural or aesthetic arguments, there are other essential and very real services that the world's ecosystems provide for us.

The great tropical forests of the world present an especially powerful case in point. As James Lovelock reminds us: *"we can be certain that the total destruction of the intricate and contrived tropical rainforest ecosystem is a loss of opportunity for all creatures on Earth."* Even in their current parlous state they are essential to the stability of the global climate. Tropical rainforests hold huge quantities of water which is released into the air through respiration. According to Rainforest Concern, more than half the world's rainwater is stored in the Amazon forests alone, with their wholesale destruction having — unsurprisingly — significant implications on the future frequency and patterns of rainfall and drought. They are also very effective 'carbon sinks', storing and consuming great quantities of carbon that would otherwise be present in the atmosphere as carbon dioxide, an important greenhouse gas driving the processes of climate change, as we are now only too aware. The deforestation of the tropics — again with reference to Rainforest Concern — is *"responsible for 18-25% of global annual carbon dioxide emissions."*

Furthermore, nature provides a vital resource as a natural pharmacy. Gone, perhaps, are the days when we sought all our cures and treatments from the wilds, but their role, especially plants, is still a crucial one, underlined by the fact that *"25% of our modern medicines originate from tropical forest plants."* Moreover, only a tiny minority of the rainforest flora has been adequately researched as regards to their pharmaceutical benefits to humans and their livestocks and pets. How many cures and treatments have slipped through our fingers before their existence was even acknowledged? Even much closer to home there are compelling examples. The leaves of the native yew, *Taxus baccata*, despite being a decidedly poisonous plant, yields compounds known as taxanes valued as an anticancer agent. Another cancer treatment is derived from the berries of the mistletoe, *Viscum album*, also poisonous, but in the right quantities useful in stimulating the immune system to deal with the rogue cells.

Even away from the iconic rainforests, with the degradation of natural habitats all over the world it is not unreasonable to assume that similarly deleterious implications are precipitating throughout and that might have an eventual effect on everyone, even if only (it seems ludicrous to use the word 'only' in this context, but hopefully you will appreciate the sentiment) in respect of ensuring the sustenance of the Earth's inhabitants. Organisms and habitats can be seen as indicators for the wider health of an ecosystem.

Things must change and indeed, in some instances, have. Before turning to my intended strand of thinking, I am given to recall, with a further digression away from the rainforests and into the oceans, a piece in *The National Geographic* a few years back, decrying the state of the world's fisheries and the imminent extinction of the bluefin tuna. As part of their coverage was an article by Kennedy Warne entitled *Blue Haven*. It concerned the establishment of a two-mile-square 'no-take' marine nature reserve at Goat Island Bay in New Zealand in the late 1970s. The all-encompassing sanctity of the reserve at the time caused great controversy with local fishermen unable to exploit the fish, mollusc and crustacean wealth of the area. The result: changes, or rather a reversal, in the marine ecology back to its more natural composition, increasing populations of fish and invertebrates within the reserve and their spilling out into the surrounding area where they could be legally caught. Happy habitat, happy fishermen, happy conservationists. We must maintain hope for widespread and sustainable change.

A digression, but a worthwhile one, and one that I will continue just long enough to return us to the wider ideas of value, need and affinity for and with the living world. It is easy enough to appreciate the value for the fisherman increasing his catch and perhaps also for the tourism of the local area – mentioned in the same article – with the "*hundreds and thousands of people a year coming to look at the fish.*" But away from this and towards the less tangible needs humans have for wildness and the idea of an affinity with nature, words and thoughts might be more difficult to align, even though such things are clearly evident to us, both individually and communally.

As individuals, we derive, at whatever level we choose, that sense of well-being from an agreeable landscape and the company of wild things around us. The wide vista of the coast might release our minds from the clamour of the everyday and its familiar routines. This could be the sight of wild geese sweeping overhead in their winter skeins or the waders billowing past in their breathtaking bird-clouds, each taking with them as they pass that part of us that yearns to fly; we relish that suggestion of the wild that they bring, even into close proximity with our urban centres. A pocket of sultry summer grassland, bounded by tall hedges that seclude the easy sway of the grasses and the scattered colours of meadow flowers; the seemingly effortless passage of butterflies – browns bouncing across the sward, blues flashing from bloom to bloom; the intense but never oppressive buzz of copious doing. All things that can calm a restless mind from its troubles and bring clarity of thought, strengthen our resolve for the rigours of everyday life, or simply engender those feelings of uncomplicated pleasantness that the open spaces can bring.

Why should this be? Such affinities, it would seem, run deep. Deeper than simply a closeness, although this most fundamental level of engagement should not be underestimated. The act of engagement is much the most significant element of the equation, rather than any sense of level or depth, or even an understanding of any mental processes involved. But the mind may nevertheless be drawn to a more all-encompassing perspective.

It is unavoidable here to lean back somewhat towards the chain of thought that ran through the previous chapter in that the motives in question are deep seated and innate. Not least with regards to James Lovelock's views of a mutually – beneficial, regulating world, with its atmosphere, oceans, organisms and rocks fine-tuning and balancing the biosphere for life to thrive. The first port of call for most, however, might instead be at that individual level. The flocks of geese, the meadow flowers and insects, all striking chords within us in different ways. Sometimes very much so (the sight of a handsome Garden Spider hanging in its patient hedgerow vigil or the silently coiled silver-black Adder absorbing the spring sun certainly have the capacity to engender polarised responses!), while others in more subtle, personal ways.

As a naturalist of getting on for 40 years (basically since I was knee high to the proverbial grassland invertebrate), I have time and time again been amazed and captivated by nature's many depths, something which I am very happy to say continues. But whilst over the years the making of lists and the pursuit of the new has delighted, it is the sense of the wholeness of all those things that has come increasingly to the fore. The requirements for my own connecting with nature could perhaps be described as contextual. That is to say I am as much a part of the process of engagement as those things of my observation, as is also the time and place in which this engagement occurs.

Different things and different places may resonate uniquely at different times. I will always long to find myself splendidly lost amid the hulking monoliths of soaring mountains, gouged with sweeping valleys in turn scoured by long-melted glaciers. I also know, however, that the same breadth of wonder, if not visual splendour, is also possible within the verdant throng of a small urban wood, with the intimate experience of its rich ecology focussed into its modest acres; the sort of space, perhaps, watched over by one of Edward Thomas's *"little gods of the earth"* that protect the small places while all around them succumb (from *Spring on Pilgrims' Way*). I am also aware that such circumstances can align themselves in the quiet solitude of my own suburban garden so that I may be enthralled and entranced by its life cycles to a similar end. And indeed, the beauty of the mountains does not reside solely within the awe of their visible presence but also within the jewels of the tiny flowers that withstand the buffeting and tantrums of the volatile upland climate, capturing droplets of rain which glisten brightly even in the murk of the 'perma-drizzle'. In the familiarity of the small birds that take just as easily to the rugged moor or wind-blasted crags as they would the mild lowland heath or tumbledown wall of some old cottage garden in the southern counties.

Such resonances are unique, not only to the place but also to the person; it is such as these, of course, that echo through much of what fills the pages of this book. Unique, yet – risking something of a contradiction in terms – not exclusive. Such experiences can be considered with an objective, yet no less impassioned mind, so that they may be reflected upon and imparted. They perhaps might not be received with the same fervour that they were offered, while at other times and for other sensibilities, they will procure the sense of place and fleeting moments, something of the visceral and the intangible. To be able to sufficiently rationalise and verbalise such vague 'on-the-tip-of-the-tongue' thoughts that can drift in and out of one's thinking, can be a frustratingly elusive thing to do, as Edward Thomas (in his book *One Green Field*) found with the field of poppies in the dawn sunlight that *"proposed impossible dreams of strength, health, wisdom, beauty, passion – could I but relate myself to them more closely than by wonder."*

It may indeed be with the writer, one who has taken some stock of their experience and relation with their surroundings and effectively expressed them to the reader, who we might look towards for a point of reference and seed of our own inspiration. Words can make us feel lost, causing us to long for situations away from our given circumstance. Yet by the same token they can ground us and keep us close to those same places that we long for. There was indeed Edward Thomas, whose air of melancholy, even if only faintly so, would often not seem far from his writings but would serve only to heighten the emotion and sense of beauty of the things and places that so often put his pen to the page. As in his book *One Green Field*, in the one breath he would lament the elusiveness of true and complete happiness and that he is *"fated to be almost happy."* In the next he declares: *"The shadow of it I seem to see every day in entering a little idle field in a sternly luxuriant country."* It is a field bounded by hedges of *"noble and fascinating unruliness."* A field *"that rises sleepily from East to West"* within which *"furze on a mound makes a little world for two or three pairs of linnets and whitethroats"* and where *"a hundred young brier stems spend spring and summer perfecting the curves of their long leaps."* A corner of the countryside where in spring those Linnets *"sprinkle a song like audible sunlight"* and where the leaves of autumn oaks *"are falling continually from those smouldering sunset clouds of foliage."* By the time he has finished composing the image of his *"little idle field"* he has made it seem like one of the happiest places on Earth.

Thomas was one of several nature writers working during the decades either before or after the turn of the 20th century that for many make the period such a rich one for the lover of natural history literature. Richard Jefferies, Thomas's hero, was another who, if not necessarily melancholic in his writings, expressed a great unease with the *"endless and nameless circumstance of everyday existence"* (*The Story of My Heart*), which served only to draw greater emphasis to a love of the countryside – its flora and fauna, people and places. He had within him a great ability for observation and description – faculties, as we have already seen, so often applied to such things that might in most people stir no more than a few words, if any at all, but that would for him warrant so many. Not only with the small details of life, so small as to often elude casual observation, but also at times concerning things concealed within the obviousness of much larger experiences. The faintly experienced character of the summer air perhaps, filling the valleys and hillsides of the South Downs; a quality of the 'atmosphere' that was *"too shadowy for the substance of a cloud, too delicate for outline against the sky, fainter than haze, something of which the eye has consciousness, but cannot put into a word to itself."* Or the very sound of the air, underlying the hum of midsummer, which

> *"besides the quivering leaf, the swinging grass, the fluttering bird's wing, and the thousand oval membranes which innumerable insects whirl about, a faint resonance seems to come from the very earth itself... it is this exquisite undertone, heard and yet unheard, which brings the mind into sweet accordance with the wonderful instrument of nature."*

(from *The Life of Fields*, 1884)

To read these authors now, a hundred or more years on, they will often feel of another age, as indeed in many respects they are. A turn of phrase, though wonderful, might seem out of date in a contemporary text. I've read of some of Thomas's early work being described as containing prose which was 'overwrought' and Jefferies would at times write with such fervour as to perhaps be guilty of the same. The way we write has changed, just as the landscapes about which we write have also changed, in some cases almost out of recognition, yet the responses that are stirred within the reader I am quite sure remain consistent.

Not all writers of the time could necessarily be described in quite such dramatic terms. W. H. Hudson wrote in his book *Hampshire Days* with an undoubted passion and no less engagingly, but his disillusionment of urban life appeared to come in the shape of good old-fashioned dislike, even once going as far to proclaim that: "*I feel 'strangeness' only with regard to my fellow men, especially in towns, where they exist in conditions unnatural to me, but congenial to them...*" Even the New Forest town of Lyndhurst wasn't spared his vitriol, describing it as he did as "*a transcript of Chiswick or Plumstead in the New Forest where it is in the wrong atmosphere... on which London vomits out its annual crowd of collectors*" – how he hated the butterfly collectors of the day.

With other writers, such discord would result only in greater clarity and heart-felt feeling for the things of nature. Hudson brought to this a satisfyingly objective tone that would encompass such things that might be more often ignored and sometimes reviled. The idea of discovering a favourite basking spot of a pair of Adder was an "*exulting thought*", so that he might be able to observe more closely their "*beautiful shining bodies.*" He loved the "*smallness and secretiveness*" of so-called pests that he would rather "*feel alive, teasing, stinging, and biting*" in the "*green and flowery places*", understanding, as he did, the place of everything in nature. While the Great Green Bush-cricket provided as much of a thrill as the wider, more commonly held beauties of the countryside: "*A colony of viridissima – what a happiness it would be to discover such a thing.*"

To stir the senses, to in some small way make tangible via the page the pure emotion of a moment and the place in which that moment happens, as these writers on many occasions achieved, is a rare talent. And sometimes it might simply be an author's attention to the subtle details of their subject and ability for apparently simple, even effortless description that establishes so lucidly that connection between the reader and the place, fleshing out the rudiments of mere ink and paper. In other words, the means to capture the small movements of things and the places where they live – their glorious mundanity and unguarded trivialities.

There are many who, with a great deal of justification, would put forward J.A. Baker's *The Peregrine* as the perfect accomplishment of just this, such is his evocation of the bird and its place, and the others among them. The bird that soared on a rising thermal with "*a steep, flickering helix, hypnotic in style and rhythm, his long wings tireless and unfaltering.*" The backdrop a veritable coastal wilderness, where "*the calmness and solitude of horizons…layer the memory like strata*"; where the "*constellations of golden plover*" are flushed high into the sky by a falcon's passing and the wings of frightened duck and starling that "*hissed the shallow air.*" Thus the man, the bird, the landscape and the elements are irreversibly intertwined.

It is a wonderful and celebrated book, but it is another author who I feel moved to make further mention of here, perhaps in part due to his apparently receiving scant reference for his literary talents. Eric Ennion (1900-81) was a writer and also a most gifted artist, mostly of birds. He evidently translated into the written word much of the talent he possessed as an artist when capturing his subjects so dynamically onto canvas. He wrote with a certain evenness, yet the meshing of the man with the land and its life, to my mind, was no less potent, and described with a quiet air of keen observation that only a deep sense of connectivity and a love for the objects of his deep fascination could provide. An autumn flock of Lapwing that "*rose…and trailed across the sky; a bunch leading the way, the rest strung out behind like a scarf caught by the wind*" are given life and movement within a mere two dozen words in his book *The Lapwing*. His beloved Cambridgeshire fenlands (which he revisits in *Adventurers Fen*) were places where "*summer dawdled into autumn*" and where the water in the ditches was "*yeasty with very small life*", where a Garganey drake slumbered in a pool amid a reed-bed that "*lay at anchor swaying as a light wind touched first on one corner and then the other.*" Thus we are immersed so easily into a sanctuary of whispering reed and silent pools, a world heavy and bristling with life that we might feel more than we see.

A Grasshopper Warbler reeling on top of a bush, somewhere in the Adventurers' Fen, sometime during the 1930s. We can see inside its open beak, into the "*translucent orange*" of its mouth. We can appreciate the effort of its singing from "*the hair-fine ticking of its cheeks*" and by the "*eyes fever bright as the slim body thrilled in ecstasy*". The bird is not merely a grammatical representation of a small, skulking animal, about 13 centimetres long, with a grey-brown, streaked plumage; in fact there is little mention of its physical attributes. It is a creature, though, with the resurgence of the spring glinting in its eye. It is a bird filled with an urgency for life, which overflows beyond the two dimensions of a page and the few seconds it takes to read of it.

I could go on to fill many pages of this book with such words as these, as well as those already quoted and the others to come, something which would justify a whole tome in itself. The choice of who would fill those pages would naturally be a deeply subjective decision. As presented above, they are intended to embellish a point. They prove to me the presence of a very real, emotional longing for people to understand something more of their place within the scheme of things. Proof of the lasting bonds we have with our natural environment, strained and obscured as they are by the obstacles of modern life placed before them. The words needed to be written and needed to be read. The reader who finds a deep resonance within them shares a great part of that which stirred such passion in their writer.

As for the author of this book, the moments and sentiments expressed by these others, be they as outpourings of unfettered emotion or as peaceful and no less sincere appreciation for natural beauty, always find a common ground. Many reading this, I am sure, would put others in their place as those who might inspire us to think further on our relationships with our environment, but from the differing points of origin that the thinker begins, each arrives at the same destination. A place where, imbuing such words with whatever properties we choose, the *spirit* would be lifted and the *soul* soothed, places of renewal and re-energisation. I, no doubt like others, bear some regrets for things I could have done differently in the past, but it is among those places where nature predominates the senses, that everything is reconciled. It is here where the anxieties of life and the causes of ire are somehow always given a truer perspective.

As powerful as our own individual ties with nature may be, in a wider sense they are not necessarily a basis for the human relationship with it, but rather an extrapolation of something more intrinsic and more fully encompassing. Our affiliations with nature through society and culture perhaps reach further into the broader aspects and collective perceptions of human life. The value of nature to the individual will obviously be subject to a degree of variability in that our views on it and interpretation of ourselves among it will naturally differ, but they may also have much in kind with the common perceptions of society, something which will arguably bring a greater influence to bear on prevailing attitudes. These, of course, do not always result in a positive long-term effect by means of human activities justified and misguided by cultural and social tradition. This is not something to be dwelt on too much here, but cultural attitudes and religious doctrines can be seen in the past (and in certain instances, some might say, with a continuing influence) to have cultivated a lop-sided, humanistic view of our 'role' in nature and our subsequent use and abuse of it, all in the name of progress and our 'rights' as human beings; the "*anthropocentric*", human-centred tendencies and the "*dominant western worldview... that nature exists for human use*" described by Johnston and Janiga (1995). But those that do not degrade might instead nurture. The values placed on nature by culture and society will also add something more to our human needs to those we have for a sustaining environment. Recognising and incorporating them into the everyday of modern life is being increasingly viewed as the way forward for the benefit of ourselves and also the future of wildlife conservation.

This is perhaps where definitions become harder to come by. It may be too crude to describe such a dilemma as of cultural value versus material value, if only in view of the fact that not everyone in the world has the luxury to consider these issues with their needs of sustenance and shelter fully satisfied; people are, after all, inextricably a part of the land themselves. Herein, though, lies the challenge for those who would seek further changes in how modern humans live in the world. A challenge that encompasses the vagaries of idealism and emotion, pinning down loose ideas and the held perceptions of places and things.

The fact that such values exist seems clear enough however. Ever since when the likes of the early-17th-century tourists to the Lake District began to appreciate the wild country as a thing of beauty rather than one of foreboding (not, mind you, without a full entourage of servants in tow to ensure plenty of home comforts!), the cultural significance of the great outdoors has come to be recognised. Much less likely now, and to refer to a pair of wonderful quotes cited by Douglas Botting in *Wild Britain*, would the wilds of Snowdonia be described as *"horrible with the sight of bare stones"* as John Leland did in the mid-16th century . Nor would the fine country of the New Forest earn the dubious distinction afforded it by William Cobbett in the 1820s of *"a poorer spot than this New Forest there is not in all of England, nor I believe in the whole world."*

Times in this respect have indeed changed. The sojourns into the wild and wonderful corners of the country are no longer just the reserve of the wealthy. It is a resource of our natural heritage accessible beyond any ideas of class, in essence at least if not in practice. The National Park Authority's own figures reveal that between them, the fifteen National Parks in England, Scotland and Wales, welcome more than 60 million visitors every year. Even if we assume that some will visit more than one National Park during a given year and that some people will visit the same park more than once during that time, such a figure bears testament to the important role the wild places of our land plays in the lives of its people. In isolation, the Peak District, Yorkshire Dales and Lake District National Parks, respectively, attract in excess of ten, nine and eight million visitors annually. The wild lands and rolling acres of pastoral tranquillity that comprise our national parks will be looked to first as the places to best provide our needs of the countryside and the presence of nature, but our country, although much less so than in the past, is threaded — albeit tenuously — with a network of opportunity for them to be met.

These needs and the significance and potential of nature in satisfying them are not always obvious: something more than the proverbial change of scenery that the millions go in search of in our National Parks each year. This is testament, once again to Bill Adams's (1996) 'cultural archive' and another example perhaps, of that exchange between people and the land, and the mark that each leaves on the other. Countless histories must bind us to the land, not only culturally but also biologically, whatever ideas of instinct and evolution that you may happen to subscribe to. If we are to take a naturalistic view of ourselves and the world, then our environment must have reciprocated our shaping influence of it (to some extent, at least, even given our current reign of havoc!) through the same ecologies that relate to any other species and its habitat.

The ties of culture have always been there which, according to Edward O. Wilson in his book *Biophilia: The human bond with other species*, "*cascade into repetitive patterns of culture across most or all societies.*" The symbolism of the snake, for example (and on which Wilson writes at length), occurs independently in the cultures of many peoples across the continents and through time. Not just the Christian tales of Adam and Eve but also as demons in China, Hindu goddesses in India, and deities to the ancient Egyptians. This he presumes to be the result of generations of unfortunate encounters with poisonous snakes, giving them a prominent place, ingrained into the cultural consciousness, manifested in the dreams and other mystic experiences to provide the stuff of myth and legend.

There are even instances of the pigeon being afforded religious significance, or at least their Rock Dove ancestors. Mesopotamian models of shrines and fertility goddesses, dated at around 6500 BP, have been discovered that prominently featured pigeons, presumably because of their "*vigorous reproductive capabilities*" (with a constant supply of food, feral pigeons today can produce up to six broods throughout the year). Some 3200 years ago, King Ramses II of Egypt is said to have made the extraordinary offering of 58,000 pigeons to the priests of Amon, the King of Gods. Birds especially, or so it seems, are common examples of such religious associations. One might need only look to the tales of folklore and religious myth that accompany Edward Armstrong's *Birds of the Grey Wind* (1944), the Celtic oystercatcher on the shores of Strangford Lough that warned Christ of his oncoming enemies and helped conceal him among the rocks and seaweed, or the legend of Zeus who assumed the form of a swan to seduce the beautiful Leda.

Some such ties are, of course, present today, not only with the wings of birds but also those of butterflies. The arrival of the Monarch migration where it concentrates in parts of Mexico is an eagerly awaited occasion for indigenous communities. In late summer the butterflies embark on an extraordinary migration that extends from Canada and the northern United States south into Central America, covering distances in excess of 3600 kilometres (2250 miles). It is a distance too great for any single Monarch to complete and they will mate and pupate during the course of the return leg of the journey there and back. It is a feat of flying that results in their regular, if infrequent storm-driven occurrence on British shores and has enabled their colonisation of the Antipodes and Pacific Islands, and the Azores and Canary Islands on the Atlantic side (alas their Milkweed food plants are neither native or widely cultivated in the UK). They hibernate/aestivate in quite staggering congregations of millions of butterflies in specifically favoured areas of coniferous forest in Mexico, so as to clothe the branches in such abundance as to look themselves like the autumn-brown leaves of deciduous trees.

Arriving at their hibernation sites, they may pass over a festival scene. Local villages cash in on the tourism that this wild spectacle brings with it, selling the full range of tourist merchandise as would be familiar the world over, providing much needed income for what are generally fairly poor farming communities. The significance of the butterflies to the people, however, has a much deeper connection than merely an opportunity to cash in. It is their belief that each butterfly is the embodied soul of a dead relative and loved one returning for 'el Dia de los Muertos' – the festival of 'the Day of the Dead'. Thus, the cycle of the Monarch's life is so very deeply ingrained into the cultural life and happiness of these communities and with the continued threat to the safety to their hibernation sites, posing the risk of both ecological and spiritual devastation. The locals are fiercely proud and protective of their butterflies.

Such are examples of the many instances of the lasting entwining of the consciousness of people and the natural world. Something that has persisted in all cultures and has precipitated almost subliminally into our thinking, even incorporating so humble and sometimes despised a creature as the pigeon. Societies and cultures have evolved always with the threads of nature woven within and will continue to do so: from the past beliefs of certain plants and animals possessing mystical potency, to the more rational modern day acceptance and appreciation of the psychological benefits of our protecting and nurturing of other life.

Our bonds with the biodiversity of the planet would certainly seem to go beyond those construed by religion or shaped by cultural attitudes. Beneath the surface of these interactions lies that deeper connection, again drawing us back to the considerations of the previous chapter. Such connections that underpin even those that take place by way of the constructs of civilisation. This is an idea so very eloquently summarised by Edward O. Wilson in *Biophilia*:

> *"To explore and affiliate with life is a deep and complicated process in mental development...our existence depends on this propensity, our spirit is woven from it, hope rises on its currents."*

The ties were there long before they ever became a focus of philosophy, so why should we ever assume that they could be broken?

Perhaps, when provided with the circumstances to have concern for the natural world and finding ourselves with a need to conserve and preserve it – to have closeness with it – we come into contact with some deeply innate sense of self-preservation as much as a sense of obligation to our fellow species. Lovelock suggests a predisposition in humans to yearn for a proper, healthy relationship with our surroundings and the things of nature that comprise the living biosphere. A situation he believed that if allowed to prevail would "*arouse the pleasurable feelings which comprise our sense of beauty*", but when disrupted might cause us to "*suffer from a sense of emptiness and deprivation.*"

Nature has and always will be an important element of human life, a relationship ever present if not necessarily straightforward; as Bill Adams identifies in his book *Future Nature*: "*We are part of nature, yet we need the 'otherness' of nature.*" While it may be important to realise our own place within it all, in order to understand this importance we must also maintain our stance as observers as well as the observed, something that in contradiction necessitates some sense of removing ourselves from that which we must be – and indeed are – a part of. Wilson asserts that other organisms "*are the matrix in which the human mind originates and is permanently rooted.*" In understanding this are we able to assume the positions of both subject and object, and a clearer impression of our needs and values and our place within nature?

As something of a footnote here, there is a final irony to be added. Our attentions have been drawn towards the holism of nature, to the things of nature as being givers and takers to the benefit of all its constituent parts and as providers of balance and stability. In addition to this, through our connection with it, the benefits of balance and stability may also be experienced within the human consciousness and indeed also, it would seem likely, the subconscious. Those simple things as to be experienced before we even begin to question why, such as hearing bird songs reverberating the spring woods, being enveloped by the abundant hum of insect life among the heaving marsh, the visual depth and warmth of flower-studded, butterfly-adorned meadow, all add a kind of counterweight to some of the falsehoods of modern life and an opportunity for equilibrium. The warblers in the wood, the insects in the marsh, and the colour and life of the meadow can profoundly affect us and change our 'take' on the world and ourselves. Yet without us in the picture, the Blackcap would sing the same song, the dragonflies would still enact their same extraordinary life cycle amidst the marshland habitat, and the flowers and butterflies would still paint the same picture of symbiosis and harmony among the sward.

Part 4

The Meaning of Things

Simple Nature

Simple nature is sitting out in the first warmth of spring, with the garden birds at the feeders oblivious to the proximity of your presence. Hearing that low, concerted buzzing and then seeing the year's first queen bumblebee emerging from the early green foliage, flying steady and purposeful as she searches the garden for a place to house her brood in waiting. It is trying to remember how small a tree was when you planted it and not being able to imagine the view from the window without it. Or a bubble, instantaneous at the surface of the pond, a glance and the flick of a newt's tail disappearing into the weedy shadows, while the vestiges of the winter chill tangs the evening air. Knowing that all of this is just the start.

Simple nature is the tiny chlorophyll fountain of a fern issuing from the mortar of a city harbour wall; Ragwort blooming brightly among the uncompromising substrate of railway track ballast; the different sounds that the wind makes in different trees. It is watching forest deer without them knowing you are there. Noticing the gulls streaming steadily to roost across a reddening autumn sky above a busy street and wondering where their wings have taken them. It is the bird's song above the roar of traffic and the stillness of the wee small hours.

Simple nature is familiar faces in familiar places. Thinking that a light has been left on overnight before realising that instead it is the rays of the morning sun filling the room. It is a butterfly on the tip of your finger, a spider's web, the surprise of a dragonfly in the November sunshine with wings that seem as fragile as the fading autumnal warmth. Scanning an empty hillside, but for the dot of soaring wings lifted over the horizon. Catching sight of winter gnats glancing the brittle January sunshine and pondering the resilience of small things.

Simple nature is our common ground.

The Meaning of Things

This is maybe something of a misleading title that could suggest a continuation of the philosophies contained within the previous two chapters. It refers , however, not so much to 'the meaning of things' in that fundamental sense, but instead in a much more subjective, less rational way and even with an element of whimsy thrown in for good measure. It is perhaps with a more light-hearted tone that I would look to end this book. The meaning of things in a more iconic context. Of the things that might instigate our questioning and fascination and which embody our yearning for deeper connections with our immediate environment and beyond. Those things that provide the sense of clarity to our feelings, our reasoning and our curiosity towards the cohabiters of the world around us. There are those aspects of nature – the plants, animals and places – that seem to demand that we study and understand them and their place. They might also reflect something of ourselves in return.

The things of nature have always been ascribed to the actions and expectations of humans and the world in which they live. They have been seen as signallers of events, portents of things to come and of future fortunes, the stuff of mythology and old wives' tales. The good luck brought to sailors who sighted an albatross (and the bad luck if the bird came to any grief), or the flushing of the 'ash before the oak' meaning we're 'in for a soak', rather than the less rainy days promised by the 'oak before the ash' suggesting that we might only be 'in for a splash'. The sacred pagan qualities of holly and ivy for their 'eternal' evergreen foliage and not forgetting, of course, the general fear and superstition spread by snakes throughout human history.

We have always looked to nature for signs of some kind. Perhaps most obviously for the passing of the year, the beating of the cosmic drum to which all things must keep time. Indeed, generations of poets have found themselves preoccupied by the coming and going of the seasons. From Homer's *Iliad* and such references as the Achean armies gathered "*as thick upon the flower-bespangled field as leaves that bloom in summer*", to Thomas Hardy's "*spectre-gray*" New Year frost in *The Darkling Thrush* (Hardy, 1997, to Ted Hughes's (1930-98) "*head-pincering gales*" and "*spill of molten ice*" (in the poem *Tractor*; Hughes, 2003) that helps make even starting a tractor on a winter morning sound like a gripping drama of man versus the elements…. The rhythm of the seasons naturally has a powerful influence on the imagination, creatively or otherwise. Who isn't drawn at some time, and not necessarily in an overly sombre context, to thoughts of introspection and reflection during the grey winter days and, more poignantly, who can fail to be uplifted by the building momentum of spring.

With Hardy's thrush still in mind, it is the birds that seem to often capture the imagination, certainly with the written word, of those wishing to establish an interface for some meaningful connection with the natural world. Keats had the Nightingale in his famous ode. A poem where the beauty of a spring wood and the bird that "*Singest of summer in full throated ease*" is used to give stark contrast to the poets troubled mind, but perhaps tinged with hope, with the fading song becoming "*buried deep / In the next valley glades*", maybe with the chance of hearing it again in happier times. Hughes (2003) had his Swift, whose reappearance each spring reassured him that "*the globe's still working*" and his '…Hawk in the Rain', the bird that "*Effortlessly at height*" tamed a raging storm. John Clare (1793-1864) wrote of the Snipe that reminded him that even in the gloom of the "*quagmire overgrown*" and the "*stagnant floods*" there would still be something of nature to lift his mood (in MacBeth, 1965):

> *"Thine teaches me*
> *Right feelings to employ –*
> *That in the dreariest places peace will be*
> *A dweller and a joy."*

(from *To The Snipe*)

The cultural, spiritual and philosophical ties between humans and birds are, and as none other than the pigeon has reminded us, as old as civilisation. In the first instance, the very fact that they can fly makes them the image of that sense of liberation, that sense of freedom – psychological, spiritual, or whatever you want to call it – that everyone has sought at some point and some way. And they are beautiful, and so marvellously diverse, all 9,000 or so of them: from the most resplendent Peacock right down to the most self-effacing, dun-coloured little warbler, each has its own wonder in its own right. What one might go by with rarely anything more than a passing glance, another might find astounding and moving, a source of endless and unrivalled fascination.

For Mark Cocker in his book *Crow Country* it was crows, in particular the Rook that in the most part filled the pages of his book *Crow Country*. Echoing the sentiments of Bill Adams in *Future Nature* and his words already quoted, Cocker recalls the maturation of his childhood interest in wildlife into something with a more weighty, more intrinsic significance – the interpretation of wild creatures as *"expressions of some new-found and compelling otherness in nature."* It appears that it was the Rooks that came to represent this most clearly, the subtleties of their behaviour and the social complexities of their lives being analogous to the similar and profound enigmas to be found throughout nature.

The crows are an engaging bunch of birds, even if only for their potential for dividing opinion. With some maybe more so than others, they are to a species a canny and resourceful group, and wholly entertaining, if only we were less inclined to view them at worst with such scornful prejudice or at best with general indifference. They are clever. Jackdaws have been known to figure out puzzles in order to gain food, Magpies are supremely adaptable and when have you ever seen a Rook or a Carrion Crow as a road kill, in spite of their scavenging behaviour? It is another member of the crow family that can, for me, embody the very essence of nature's frivolity when it takes leave from its harsh but wonderful realities. Watching a party of Ravens tumbling and 'playing' on a rising thermal can extend the invigoration of the uplands even higher and beyond the heather and stone. If anyone resists the idea that we humans are not the only animals capable of properly experiencing joy, just watch such a display of plunging stoops, mid-air back-flips, airborne twists and their various other gratuitous aerobatics, surely you will be convinced or at least offer the whole question more thought. There seems no obvious function beyond the presumed social bonding that such activities allow — something, it should be remembered, that could reasonably be said of our own social and recreational behaviour. They offer physical form to the sense of elation we experience ourselves when among the wild country and an extension of the sense of freedom that pervades the wide open spaces into the boundless expanse of the sky. It is not often that a crow is looked to for such a celebration of a landscape, but the Raven transformed from lumbering groundling into aerial acrobat is, I believe, a wondrous thing.

Perhaps it is their more 'human' qualities that in part engenders so much derision from so many. Indeed, it could be said that the once widespread Raven has been pegged back and persecuted to its upland strongholds because of its wily resourcefulness and perceived interference with our own manipulation of the countryside. And the fact that the Magpie, so despised for its unsavoury methods of acquiring food, is thus derided because somewhere within us it strikes a chord with the discomfort we have for the activities of our own species? It is a bird variously accused of being 'evil' and 'murderous' which, seeing as it is simply doing what it must to make its living, just as we and every other animal must, smacks very much of the pot calling the kettle black. There is only really one animal that is truly capable of being evil and it isn't the Magpie. We should perhaps take a leaf out of W. H. Hudson's book (*Hampshire Days*) and a lesson in objectivity, when he writes not of crows but of such irritating creatures as the incessantly buzzing flies that crowded a spot beside a forest stream: "*even when they came in legions about me...It was delightful to see so much life – to visit it and sit down with them in their own domestic circle.*"

Food for thought maybe, but it seems that the crows, for good or bad, perhaps *mean* something to people more than many other birds. With the names of our settlements bearing frequent reference to crows, it seems that this has long been the case – from Crowborough to Crowton, Ravendale to Rookhope, and from Crawcrook to Crawley ('crawe' being Old English for crow) it appears that we have been rather obsessed with them over the ages.

To some extent, Cocker's Rooks are my bumblebees. The Rooks represented in many respects the landscapes in which he and they existed; he tells us that "*they were a route into the landscape and my rationale for its exploration.*" Rather than the oscillation of insect activity within the rhythms of the spring and summer, it is the spectacle of the vast flocks of corvids streaming back to roost and the many and various nuances of their behaviour that, for him, instigate the slight shifting of perspective. On one occasion he admits that "*it was as if I were seeing them now for the first time.*" Similarly, even after many years as a naturalist and following my closer observation of bumblebees, they assumed to my mind a slightly altered presence within the wild places I spent time in. Such a subtle, but potentially profound change in how we see the world is something that could be described as rather like peering through a stand of trees, unable to locate the object of one's curiosity. Just a small step to one side or the other reveals a whole part of the wood that is — in a very literal sense — there all along, but hidden from sight.

If not crows or bumblebees, there will always be the more obvious candidates demanding our attention from the outset. What better than the Golden Eagle to give wings and graceful mobility to the equally awe-inspiring splendour of the sweeping glens and rock-fastened Scottish wildernesses over which they survey? A place also where the Red Deer hold sway, so often afforded the superlatives of majesty as is given also to the valleys and mountainsides on which they tread. When beside the river, is it not the blue shard of a passing Kingfisher that so many of us hope to glimpse above all else? A bird surely without rival in its embodiment of the river water, the sun-glanced riverside trees and all their jewel-like sparkle and gleam. Of the beings of the sea, it is the dolphin, parting the ocean currents and leaping so gleefully above the waves with such little apparent effort that so many yearn to see for themselves in their lifetime. And what other tree befits the long and steeped history of the British countryside better than the English Oak, so steady in its growth, so sturdy in its stature and so generous in its giving of sustenance to so many other organisms? Even the scientific name, *Quercus robur*, recalls the robustness and, literally, the strength (*robur* is Latin for strength) of these wonderful trees.

Consideration of the origins of the scientific names of species could in itself be regarded as unlocking the 'meaning of things' in its most literal sense. It is to the 18th-century Swedish naturalist Carl von Linné (or Linnaeus as he is more widely known) that we owe the currently used and universally accepted system of so-called binomial nomenclature. It is a system that is hugely helpful and essential in dispelling any confusion with the common names that may vary from region to region. What the English have tended to call the Grey Phalarope, a small winter bird that we only see here in its muted winter garb, is better described as the Red Phalarope in Iceland where they breed and are seen in their more vibrant summer plumage. But whether in England, Iceland or anywhere else for that matter, it is always *Phalaropus fulicarius*.

Plants and animals had their scientific names before Linnaeus, long-winded and cumbersome, such that species were described using whole phrases, or even sentences, relating to their behaviour and appearance. As such, the Mallard was once referred to scientifically as *Anas platyrhynchos altera sive clypeata Germanis dicta*, which translates as 'another duck with a broad bill or, according to the Germans, with a shield-like gorget'. Linnaeus proposed a far simpler alternative, using only two terms. The first related to the genus to which the organism belongs, the second assigns it as an individual species distinguishable from its relatives in the same genus. The Mallard has thus since become *Anas platyrhynchos* – "a duck with a broad bill". This laid the foundations for a beautifully simple and universally accepted system of arranging the living world.

But aside from the taxonomic benefits of such a system, scientific names can offer an impression of the habits and appearance of an organism before we have even laid eyes on it. A collection of books written by R.D. Macleod in the 1950s provide interesting and intriguing references to the origin and meaning of names. The first, generic part of a name is usually derived from Greek, whilst the specific term most often derives from Latin. Most of the time these terms are descriptive, for example in the case of the Tiger moths, the generic name *Arctia* is taken from *arctos*, the Greek word for hairy, pertaining to the furry appearance of the caterpillars. Frequently they may be descriptive, but not in an immediately obvious way. The beautiful Columbine, or *Aquilegia vulgaris*, takes its generic name (with *vulgaris* meaning common) from the Latin *aquila*, eagle, with reference to the supposedly talon-like spurs of the ornate flowers. This is also an instance where the common name tells something of a story. Columbine comes from the Latin *columba*, dove, the five-spurred petals being thought to recall a circle of inward-facing doves.

The names may be only partially revealing, however. Linnaeus, when seeking to arrange and name the butterflies, for example, often looked to the figures of Greek mythology. Thus we ended up with such wonderfully named species as *Lysandra bellargus* (although recently reclassified as *Polyommatus bellargus*) – the Adonis Blue. *Lysandra* was an Egyptian princess and daughter of the Greek prince Ptolemy. *Bellargus* is derived from *bellus* meaning beautiful (from the stunning blue of the male butterfly) and *argus*, from *Argos* the hundred-eyed monster (referring to the numerous eye spots that adorn the underwing). The result, certainly with the butterflies, is the presence of a kind of poetic romanticism that continues to accompany one of science's great milestones. Thus we also have the little Silver-spotted Skipper, *Hesperia comma*, named after the Hesperides – 'Nymphs of the Evening' – and overseers of Hera's orchard and her precious, immortality-giving golden apples, the Peacock, *Aglais io*, after Io, a priestess of Hera, the goddess of women, and the unassuming Small Blue, *Cupido minimus*, after the god of erotic love and desire!

With our 'emblems' in mind once again, it is true to say that for each one of those easy choices there are many more whose iconic qualities may be less obvious to the more popular gaze, whatever the etymology of their names. Below the soaring eagles and feet of the handsome Red Deer, there is the surreptitious skulk of what some might view as 'lesser' creatures in 'lesser' places, and while the possibility of leaping dolphins tantalise the hopeful scanning of the waves, the oceans and their terrestrial interfaces co-exist full of oddity and enigma. Beneath the spread of the oak crown a suite of other plants vie for light and space that might equally capture the mood of the countryside, and for each jewel of the waterways there are any number of rough diamonds that add their own kind of sparkle.

All are jewels in their own right. Ted Hughes (2003) certainly had an eye for the unearthed gem and the astute observation with which to polish and make them shine. With his subjects he could instil within them something of their place and their time, so that even a cranefly (in *A Cranefly in September*) "*blundering*" from "*collision to collision*" contained the very substance of the fields in early autumn, along with the "*The frayed apple leaves, the grunting raven, the defunct tractor / Sunk in nettles*". And also that a pair of Tortoiseshells (in *Two Tortoiseshell Butterflies*) – "*she drunk the earth-sweat, and he / Drunk with her*" – enacting their courtship routines to bodily carry a snow-strewn May from the unseasonal grip of winter back towards the warmth of spring.

In his *Hawk Roosting* it seems as if the bird of the title – which to my mind's eye is a Sparrowhawk – is afforded not just a moment and a point in space, but with "*the whole of Creation*" required to produce its "*foot*" [and] "*each feather*" – a foot, no less, that will come to "*hold creation*" within it. The hawk is a kind of pinnacle of the wood over which it surveys. Each thread weaving among the trees down below corresponds back to the bird, all things lead to its end.

Elizabeth Bishop (1911-1979) achieves something similar with her poem *Sandpiper* (in Hughes and Heaney, eds., 1982), although with less of the drama of Hughes's hawk. It is no less a point of focus amidst its place of habitation, but rather than presenting a pinnacle in the sense of the hawk, it provides a sort of rationalisation of the vastness and unwavering action of the ocean. The bird unaware of such magnitudes distils the character and movement of the endless, rolling sea into its few grams of flesh and feathers. There is the indifference to "*the *roaring alongside that he takes for granted*", and of the action of the waves it is only the part which "*glazes over his dark brittle feet*" that he pays any attention as he "*stares at the dragging grains.*" One could describe the ocean as it is seen spreading away to the horizon, rising and falling, and breaking onto the shore, or one could imbue the qualities of its sights and sounds and its meeting with the land into this little bird, this stop-start anomaly along the sweep of flat sand of a wave-washed beach.

The focal point might be seen to embody the wider landscape of these poems. The sandpiper is a small piece of the ocean and the hawk of the wood. There is, though, a sense of reciprocation. The sea needs its sandpipers, and its gulls hanging themselves up on the wind over the white crests of the waves, and the black shapes of its Cormorant sliding into the water and out of sight. The wood needs its bird of prey, its secret treetop butterflies, its stands of Foxgloves thrusting from the woodland floor in the sunny glades. It needs the oddity of its mushrooms poking up through the leaf litter and the songs of Blackbird and Robin winding and weaving among its trees, as much indeed as all these things themselves need the wood itself. Even an autumn field might need its craneflies to be so.

The eagles, kingfishers, dolphins and deer all have their eulogies for the beauty that they bring to their beautiful places, which should quite rightly continue to be seen and heard. But what of those more personal choices that will be more easily overlooked and which will add that much more to the substance of our experience. Others with a presence, if we are attuned to it, no less assertive to our senses and with meaning no less significant to our interpretation of the world around us. It seems appropriate to offer up some candidates for such acknowledgement. The choice of the plants and animals in the sketches below are notable in their differences but are connected by that common notion of not necessarily being the most obvious. However, with the quotes accompanying my own words, I am clearly not alone in my affections. Probably anyone reading these sketches will at times be in agreement as to some of what is written below, but equally may be dismayed at some obvious omissions.

A Season's Call

The Chiffchaff is the bird that, for me, brings the spring to these islands, yet it does not occupy a place within the human consciousness as other birds do. We do not say things like: "*It takes more than one Chiffchaff to make a summer.*" Such occasional poems as John Clare's *The Pettichap's Nest* aside, neither are they often the objects of a poet's muse, although Edward Thomas did mention them, in prose rather than in his poetry, as one of the early signs of the season that he hoped to see during his *Pursuit of Spring* that took him by bicycle across the southern counties of England. But, as far as I am aware, there has been no ode dedicated to them and no-one has ever extolled anything like: *the Chiffchaffs are back, the globe's still working*, as Ted Hughes did of the Swift (in *Swifts*, Hughes, 2003). Yet, there is surely no clearer voice to announce a season's change.

They are actually wintering in the more southerly reaches of Britain and Ireland in increasing numbers, but migrants from around the Mediterranean and from Africa, south of the Sahara, mean that numbers soar from a winter population, according to the RSPB, of no more than 1,000 to around 800,000 come the spring. This is an influx that reaches all corners of the land, barring only the north-westerly extremes of Scotland. Most of us will encounter them as a creature of spring and summer, rather than one of the winter wood. As a diminutive, green-brown shape among the treetops, it doesn't have the verve or the sheen of the swallow, swooping ashore with a style that belies what might have been as much as a 12,000-kilometre journey from Africa. With an uncomplicated, two-note song, it doesn't exactly caress the branches with a bubbling overflowing of birdsong, like the Blackcap or Nightingale. Yet their presence fills the winter-vacated spaces at least as wholly.

With a small irony, they arrive in our woods with the very last days of winter yet to pass and the trees still bare of leaves. Ironic, for the first part of their scientific name, *Phylloscopus*, which means 'leaf-explorer'. For the leaves they must wait, but they have other means, without a need for the bright colours and elegance possessed by others, to bring life back to them and to lift that sense of a season gathering pace. Two notes is all they have, but two notes is all they need to fill the trees with a resounding aural accompaniment to the fresh optimism of spring and to the celandines blooming brightly along the stream banks and the swelling buds beginning to tint the woods.

Come mid-March and I am waiting, listening out for a faint sound somewhere in the distance. *Chiff-chaff, chiff, chiff, chiff-chaff, chiff-chaff.* Few sounds will lift the winter-weary spirits more. Listening to this proudly simple song, W.H. Hudson (in *A Traveller in Little Things*), thinking of the *"the sweet season which brings new life and hope"*, also made note of *"how a seal and sanction is put on it by that…small bird's clear and resonant voice."* Regardless of what wintry outburst the British climate might still dish out, once this little bird has cast its notes across the countryside the spring can only recoil so much. Of the same sound Thomas wrote in *In Pursuit of Spring*, *"Nothing so convinces me, year after year, that Spring has come and cannot be repulsed, though checked it may be, as this least of songs."* The c*hiff-chaff, chiff-chaff,* rebounding brightly off of the leaf-bare boughs, reverberating around the waking wood, is the sound that does so much to draw the spring out of itself, to usher in its unfolding. This is the bird that sings the spring's opening throes as loudly and as clearly as any other.

And that cyclist did hear his birds all along his journey, recalling for the reader the roadside Hampshire copses and *"the Chiffchaff that sang there, and seemed to own them."*

Spring Green

From a bird to the branches of a tree from which it might well sing and another image of the spring. For much of that season and the summer to follow, the Hornbeam is a tree of the shadows, filling the understory in the lea of the ancient woodland canopy in the south-eastern quarter of the UK. Alan Mitchell describes it as a tree that is *"pleasant, if rather dull"*. For me it is one of the unsung treasures of the woodland spring.

In truth, they never fully lose all of their aesthetic finery, even during winter's depths. After a splendid blaze of fiery autumn orange they might hold onto their browned leaves well into the winter, perhaps even a handful until the following spring. Clustered and curled, this stubborn foliage provides the perfect nooks and crannies for the tiny spiders and other invertebrates that somehow stick out the worst of the winter cold, to the relief of the equally hardy Goldcrest and Wren – insectivores with a job to survive come the depths of winter. The dark, grey-brown bark is smooth and, coated with the verglas of a crisp cold morning, will glisten in the winter sunshine. Old trees become deeply furrowed, fluted and full of character.

The timber beneath the bark is very dense and hard, the hardest of all European trees in fact. It has long been favoured by those who required a tough and unyielding material for their needs: a truncheon for a policeman, a chopping block for a butcher, strong spokes for a wheelwright, cogs for a miller. Because of their usefulness (it also makes very good charcoal) most of the Hornbeam trees encountered in British woods are multi-stem coppice stools, shaped by the cycle of decades and sometimes centuries of cutting and re-growth. In places pollards may be found, trees that were, in effect, 'coppiced' three or so metres up the trunk so as to ensure the subsequently arising shoots emerged away from the nibbling teeth of browsing mammals like deer. They do make fine old trees, but relatively few will be seen to grow into a full, domed crown, rising 20 metres or more above the ground.

It is in spring, nevertheless, that the Hornbeam comes into its glory. Useful they are too, for the tiny creatures that will help make the woodlands buzz with life. They are no 'oak', in terms of ecological productivity, but have more than 80 invertebrate species known to be associated with them. With the buds still swelling on the loftier trees above and yet to cast a shade across the woodland floor, it is they that flush with new leaves of such freshness that when bathed in the clean light of the spring sunshine their colour seems almost to possess a kind of liquid quality. They haze the subdued hues of winter tiredness with a purposeful green, obliterating the wintry wood and repairing it into a place fit to accommodate the return of the Chiffchaff and the other migrants to follow. It is a green that I'm not sure has many equals and, certainly, none more exuberant or more vibrantly toned with the optimism of the season ahead. Even beneath the inevitable spring rains and occasional relapses towards the grey of those pseudo-wintry skies, they will still glow with an unperturbed phosphorescence.

The flush of the Hornbeam is by no means the first of the season's sights and sounds to be observed within the wood. There is the aforementioned bird of course, but whereas he gives body and sound to the spring arriving, when the Hornbeam leaves begin to show, the tree offers a sign that in a way it never left but remained latent and gathering itself for the next time. A reminder that nature is never truly still but ever-restlessly working through its cycles and tracing its patterns throughout and within, around and across the land. That even in the gloomiest depths of winter, the very antithesis of the vibrancy of spring, on some scale, whether large or small, nature is always doing something, if only in preparation of events to come. The Wood Anemone will have scattered the greening carpet of brown leaves with white flowers before the buds break in earnest above them to begin the succession of spring colour across the woodland floor, but what a fitting firmament the Hornbeam provides to the spectacle.

Workaday Wings

Like that aforementioned little bird, the Buzzard comes up against some stiff competition from the others of its kind for widespread public affection. Arguably, no bird of prey in our country can match the Golden Eagle in terms of how it captures the essence of the wild and wonderful lands that they inhabit. Not many other raptors would have any answer to the sheer finesse and sublime agility on the wing than a Hobby in pursuit of such equally fleet-winged prey as Swallows, Swifts and martins. Neither are there many others that cut such a distinctive, sculpted figure as a Kestrel hovering steadfast and intent in the streaming air. The Buzzard, it could be said, appears to lack anything in the way of special and specific attributes towards the lifestyle of a top predator. In Ted Hughes's poem of the same name (*Buzzard*) (Hughes, 2003), he describes it as being "*too low-born*" for the high-speed extravagances of the peregrine and "*too dopey*" for the feats of predatory agility performed by a Sparrowhawk in pursuit of its small avian prey.

But in the case of the Buzzard, it is these very facts that brings the bird before at least one person's affections – mine; its air of adaptability and an almost 'bear-like' propensity for acquiring a decidedly varied diet. Rabbits are their mainstay, but they will also prey on birds, reptiles and amphibians, plus insects and earthworms, and all the while are not averse to a bit of carrion, especially to help them endure the winter months. Hughes's poem paints a somewhat harsh but affectionate portrait of the Buzzard. With its "*broad workaday hands / Darkened with working the land*", the image is straight away a bird without the graces of its cousins, one that grafts its way about the landscape without the luxury of specialist equipment or technique. But it is this kind of rustic grittiness that allows them to thrive in the wide open countryside of mountain, moorlands, and the wind-blasted farmlands of the cliff-top coasts that appeals so greatly.

They are one of the few raptorial birds to have increased their range over recent years towards their former extent, in spite of continued persecution. This followed the result of the myxomatosis-induced decline of rabbits in the 1950s, after which numbers halved. It is a bird that personally I have seen a great many times and each time as welcomed as the last. The Buzzard is another of those 'completers of pictures'; like a single Great Crested Grebe fishing out in the middle of a vast, sparkling mountain lake, or the stillness of a summer-silent forest momentarily rippled by a Roe Deer slipping heedlessly across the ride. It is unfair to refer to them as some kind of 'poor person's eagle'; they possess the grandness that any large bird of prey does and assume a similarly imperious presence within their landscapes. They are a substantial bird, approaching 60 centimetres in length with a wing span of well over a metre. Anyone who has seen one at close quarter, perhaps perching on an old stone wall or atop a telegraph pole watching as cars pass beneath it, would, or certainly should, have been impressed by the stature of the bird, that rugged and ruffled sort of stateliness.

They will always be a creature that signifies the wide open countryside. Buzzards are not commonplace where I live (although certainly becoming increasingly more so) and to see one always gives me that sense that I am somewhere else, away from the normal pressures of life. Even if I did ever move into 'buzzard country', or indeed if they became a common sight around where I live now, I am not sure these feelings would significantly weaken. Fortunately, Buzzards are spreading back into many of their former lowland haunts but will always remain, to my mind, a bird of the uplands and of the rolling fields, of dry-stone walls and littering scree. Even if just as a small shape circling high above the hill crest, such vistas are more complete for that speck in the sky.

Lost and Found

As part of the ongoing surveying of the flora and fauna of the environmental education centre where I worked, I found myself one September evening sitting out in the mild night air with two others watching an assortment of insects homing in on the light of a moth trap. This trap comprised a mercury-vapour bulb, a white sheet laid out on the ground and a pile of old egg boxes. The moths (along with caddis flies, shield bugs, craneflies and bush crickets…), on being drawn to the light, often scrambled amongst the recesses of the egg boxes for shelter. The owner of the trap was Don, a gentleman of considerable experience and expertise in all things lepidopteran and a name well known in Essex entomological circles.

It turned out to be a quiet night for moths, although I, perhaps with my expectations somewhat lower than that of my companions, was perfectly happy with the evening's count, with a number of new species for the Centre list and also a couple for myself, including a very beautiful specimen of a Figure of Eight. Conversation, as you might imagine, consisted largely of things entomological. With talk turning to butterflies, it emerged that in the 1950s Don was the first to see a Speckled Wood in Essex after their disappearance from the county some 30 or 40 years previously. This, it might seem to some, is not a particularly remarkable revelation, but on this evening it was one that got me thinking. The butterfly is now widely distributed across Essex, much as they are throughout the greater part of England, pretty much all of Wales and Ireland, and even increasing in northern England and Scotland where they are still a local species. Throughout my life I have only ever known woods with Speckled Woods in them. The idea that it could ever have been any different did seem rather odd.

I was aware of their chequered history of the last hundred years or so. By the early part of the 20th century this previously common and widespread butterfly had declined dramatically, to the extent that it had become largely confined to a scattering of sites in the south-west of England, Wales and western Scotland. Beginning with an increase that began back in the 1920s, it seems really quite extraordinary for it to have regained so much of its former ground in a relatively short period. In spite of all I had read before, I had till then never met anyone who had experienced first-hand a time without the Speckled Wood. To do so, and to think of its former tribulations in a slightly different, fresher light, reminded me just how lucky we are to have these delightful little creatures so widely at large in our woodlands.

They are always appreciated, of course, and fit very comfortably into the 'isn't it great that they're common' category of plants and animals, which indeed would quite easily accommodate the other species on this list. Our woods – certainly my local woods – would seem strange without them. I would say that, beyond the general fascination I have with practically every form of wildlife that I have come across, I have always had a soft spot for them. Why this butterfly more so than say a Comma, whose vibrant orange-brown in the warmth of a late February 'spring' day, is as much an antidote for the winter drear as any, I cannot say, nor the Peacock – simply stunning – or any other for that matter?

Naturally, I am thrilled by the sight of them all, but the Speckled Wood has that air of an 'old friend' about it. I have, after all, grown up with them. They may be no Peacock or Comma. They don't portray the elegance of a Swallowtail (but then how many others do?), nor the dash of the White Admiral, but what they do bring to a woodland walk is an element of companionship, of comfortable familiarity. The romantic might find elements of this within the old names that were familiar to the 18th-century naturalists. The 'Enfield Eye' would have watched walkers pass through the now forgotten woods of that district after which it was named...or the 'Wood Argus': the watchful guardian, as we might find it defined in the dictionary. After Argos, the unfaltering protector of the priestess Io of Greek mythology, the second part of this name was once much more commonly coined for butterflies with eyed wing markings.

But the Speckled Wood was the name that stuck and fitting it is too. The flicker of wings in and out of the shafts of sunlight blazing down through a space in the tree canopy is one of my quintessential visions of the summertime wood. So too the sight of rival males in dispute, spiralling around each other as if attached by some invisible, elastic thread, spinning away, up among the treetops or among the leaf-laden branches that fill the gloom of the understorey, seemingly lost in abandon for where they might end up. And they do possess a beauty in their own right. Dark, warm brown wings, speckled with creamy yellow spots, are the image of the dappled woodland sunlight that they so much enjoy. They frequent a variety of open habitats, so long as plenty of tall trees are present, such as parks, hedgerows and gardens, but like the White Admiral and the oak-top-dwelling Purple Hairstreak, the Speckled Wood is essentially a true woodland butterfly. Like the Hairstreak, the adults (needing only grasses on which to lay their eggs) also partake of the aphid honeydew coating the crowns of large trees, usually taking nectar from flowers early and late in the season when aphid productivity is at its lower ebb.

The presence of the Speckled Wood, fluttering up on your approach and settling to bask again a few metres along, is a reassuring one, an optimistic sign that things in the wood are working properly. They will be in for the duration; an early-April signal of spring's intent and perhaps an October, or certainly a late-September flourish to help ease us into the autumn. And to think — as improbable as it might seem now — they very nearly disappeared from our woods altogether, including from *my* woods. I am very glad they are back.

A Sturdy Countenance

Those flower-jewelled fields, those sweeps of petal-filled downland turf, if one should happen upon them, are truly one of the great delights of the countryside. They are delights that nowadays are all too rare. They would present an almost bewildering array of choice for anyone wishing to select a single species that might distil the mood of such a place. One could look to the vivid yellow clumps of Bird's-foot Trefoil swelling out of the sward or the simple beauty of the deep pink Grass Vetchling blooms dotted among grass stems, with their own eponymous leaves indistinguishable among the blades. Maybe the relentlessly cheerful faces of Ox-eye Daisy or the purple haze of Knapweed, rising as high as the tops of the grasses alongside which they stand. The splendour of the orchids – the springtime purple heads of Green-winged, the long, soft pink spikes of the Common Spotted later on, the deep summer pink of the Pyramidal – arguably offer some of the more obvious choices. All of these would have a strong case for selection, but it is towards another, so very familiar plant that I find myself focusing.

It is towards the rather more homely Red Clover, no less, that these attentions are drawn. Few wild flowers would be more well known. It will so often have a presence in almost any kind of grassland — meadows, along grassy roadside verges, unkempt corners of the garden and along sunny woodland rides. It is near ubiquitous to any grassy habitat and it is just this that first endears the plant to me; the fact that, more often than not, it is rarely growing much of a distance away from where one happens to be walking. It is colourful, charming and almost always around. To describe a flower as charming can sometimes be a way of acknowledging its... well, its charms, whilst also accepting that it might not be extraordinary or extravagant – the clover versus the orchid perhaps. They may not dazzle, but their flowers are certainly not dull. To see a field full of clover flowers washing a haze of purple among the green sward is to set eyes on a fine spectacle in its own right. This is something that has not been ignored as an occasional poetic muse. John Clare, in *To a Red Clover Blossom* wrote of a flower of "*lushy red*" and of "*ruddy pride*", while Emily Dickinson (1830-86) described blooms in *The Purple Clover* that were "*...ruddier than the Gown / Or Orchis in the Pasture / Or Rhododendron worn.*"

Then there are the insects. Wherever clover covers the ground, the hum of insects will fill the air above it, so prolific a source of nectar and pollen that they provide; as Dickinson aptly observed: "*There is a flower that bees prefer, / And butterflies desire*". It is such a generous little plant. Tiny flowers in their dozens, crammed into that distinctive, spherical inflorescence and so doted upon by the bearers of eager probosciscs. Clovers are a key component of bumblebee foraging habitat and rarely without the attentions of a host of other bees and numerous other insects. The leaves too are inevitably also much sought after. The stunningly iridescent Narrow-bordered Five-spot Burnet (one of those few instances where the common name is more of a mouthful than the scientific one); the filigree-winged Latticed Heath; the strikingly patterned Mother Shipton, Burnet Companion and the Shaded Broadbar; all-day flying moths that number the Red Clover among their food plants. And others also. The Chalk Carpet and Common Heath, the Heart and Club and Garden Dart, and a host of micro-moths, all lay their eggs on the crescent-marked leaves. There is the Pea Weevil whose larva feed on the root nodules, and even a tiny fly called *Agromyza nana*, just a few millimetres in length, whose grubs mine the inside of the clover's foliage. Its place in the countryside had been noticed by multitudes well before human attentions were drawn to it.

To the naturalist, a propensity for attracting other wildlife will always be well received, but like all others in the pages of this chapter, it is something of the character of the plant that brings it towards the forefront of my affections. Yes, there is its ubiquity and also the generosity that makes it is so appealing to the entomologist within me, but there is something more to it. There is, I think, a sense of resilience to this low-growing plant that is very much overlooked. The hardiness manifested in its ever-presence:

> *"She doth not wait for June;*
> *Before the World be Green*
> *Her sturdy little Countenance*
> *Against the wind — be seen."*

(from *The Purple Clover*)

Indeed, after the summer-time thunderstorm has battered the meadow grasses to an angle, the clovers among them always seem to remain unflustered by the pounding from the rain.

These are all strong claims to make on behalf of what might be perceived as a rather humble little plant, but which for me are unjust. Does it also carry with it a little bit of hope, hope that even with the demoralising losses and shameful paucity of the flower-strewn grassland habitats, there are species that will carry the colour and richness of such places until — hopefully — better times arise?

Different Folks...

A warm Tuesday afternoon during late spring in London's East End. I am walking through Mile End Park, close to the centre of the London Borough of Tower Hamlets. It is busy with people, mostly young people, but also the odd dog-walker and those stretching their legs, perhaps using the park as part of a route encompassing the relative quiet of the nearby canals and their unlikely coots. It is not a location that is given over to wildlife in any immediately obvious way (although a short time spent will of course reveal the unkempt corners and kindly motives) and is unlikely to feature in many 'where to see wildlife' guides. This is not without some reason. I see or hear little of the wild creatures that I am sure do find their niches here. It is nearly 5pm and the noise of the traffic ascending to its rush hour would certainly have drowned out many of the smaller noises emanating from the park, although not the twitter of Goldfinch somewhere overhead.

I walk past a group of trees (under which someone has delightfully seen fit to plant a scattering Snake's-head Fritillary) that merge into a denser cover of airy scrub. Some teenagers are sat on a circle of logs, so I decide not to wander among the trees and bushes; not for any sense of threat – there is none at all – but rather a sense of keeping myself to myself. Perhaps there is even a vague air of self-consciousness, if I were to begin inspecting the blossoming thorn for nectaring insects, so close to where they sat, although I am, of course, quite happy with the eccentricities of my passions and the ostensibly odd behaviour that they can lead to.

The park is busy with busy people. Not with loafing groups of dope-smoking twenty-somethings or swearing teenagers bereft of adjectives, which certain parts of the popular press might have us believe. But with kids playing football and some being put through their paces around the running track. I look between the boughs of a line of trees where the grass is allowed to grow long at their roots and see a few lads playing cricket. There are two girls messing about beneath the branches of tall tree; I didn't think to check which kind – it was an evergreen, perhaps some sort of cedar. One girl is swinging on one of the lower branches. I hear a crack and the branch yields to her weight. She did not mean to break it and leaves it be and doesn't try to finish the job, as I confess I was anticipating she would. The tree briefly takes on an almost paternal demeanour, as if it is content with the sacrifice of a small part of its being for the pleasure it gives to those in its presence and the significance of its place in the park; it's not the first time and it won't be the last.

I am not so naïve as to think that such an area as this does not have its social problems, as indeed many places do, and would not wish to insult its residents with any sort of ill-informed, middle-class flippancy. But most of the kids are just kids, adapting to their environment as they must. Neither am I going to attempt to conjure up an exaggerated sense of 'belonging' and 'community', intensified by the realities of inner-city life based on some romanticised suburban whim (although for all I know in some instances such an exaggeration may well not be necessary). But the bustle of doing, of people being outside and absorbing the warmth of a sunny spring day, expresses the sense of value that people place on these open spaces, whether consciously or not; it is a value more easily taken for granted the greater the opportunities we have to access it.

I don't expect there were many other naturalists in the park that day, although one must never be too presumptuous, but I do think that most of the people were there for essentially the same reasons as the naturalist, or for that matter, anyone else with a passion for the outdoors. To realise that need for green that lays rooted within all of us. To feel the sun on the skin and a surface beneath the feet more yielding than the concrete that can prevail so greatly. A response to the things that triggers in all of us a need to find space filled in some way with green, living things, even if so closely shared by others. It is only proper that a child should be able to enjoy such as this without pausing to question why and to be able to take it, in a sense, for granted, but I bet I was not the only one who smiled at the fritillaries beneath the trees that day.

This in a sense provides something of a bottom line, an edge – I hope – of common reality to the sentiments and philosophies contained in this book, such that perhaps only a certain level of comfort in life allows one the time and inclination to consider. There is, after all, so much that I have already taken for granted. At the end of the day it is important to just be and to dispense with any hierarchical notions of knowledge interpreted as a 'greater' experience. If knowing about the component parts of the natural world is your way of refining your experience of 'just being', then you must continue to immerse yourself in the constantly unfolding wonder of it all. But it is a relative thing. If you just need to lie on the grass, with the sun on your face and with a little space for your head to free itself for a while from its urban trappings and the demands that that brings, then that is what you must do; you will most probably notice them, but you may or may not become inquisitive as to the identities of the different butterflies that flutter past as you recline or the birds that briefly score the perfect blue overhead. At the fundamental level the net gain is the same, relative to the given need at the given time.

Me personally, I love to sit and feel warmed by the sun and grass beneath me, but I will always be inquisitive of the butterflies that go by and bumblebees and the birds and the hoverflies and the …

Acknowledgements

Special thanks to Ted Benton for writing the foreword to this book.

I am also most grateful for the professional advice and editorial input from Hugh and Nicola Loxdale at Brambleby Books.

Bibliography

Adams, W.M. (1996) *Future Nature*. London: Earthscan.

Armstrong, E.A. (1944) *Birds of the Grey Wind*. London: Lindsay Drummond.

Baker, J.A. (1967) *The Peregrine*. London: Collins.

Benton, T. (2000) *Bumblebees of Essex*. Wimbish: Lopinga.

Botting, D. (1992) *Wild Britain*. London: Sheldrake Press.

Brown, W.G. (1947) *My River*. London: Frederick Muller.

Brownjohn, A., Hamburger, M., Tomlinson, C. (eds.) (1969) *Penguin Modern Poets 14*. Harmondsworth: Penguin.

Clare, J. as sourced from www.johnclare.info

Cocker, M. (2008) *Crow Country*. London: Vintage.

Dickinson, E. (1830-1886) *The Purple Clover*, found on www.oldpoetry.com.

Ennion. E.A.R. (1949) *The Lapwing*. London: Methuen and Co.

Ennion, E.A.R. (1996) *Adventurers Fen*. Cambridge: Colt Books.

Gagliardo, A. *et al.* (1999) Homing in Pigeons: The Role of Hippocampal Formation in the Representation of Landmarks Used for Navigation. *The Journal of Neuroscience*, 1999, *19*(1):311-315.

Gagliardo A. *et al.* (2001) The ontogeny of the homing pigeon navigational map: evidence for a sensitive learning period. *Proc Biol Sci*. 2001; 268(1463): 197-202

Grigson, G. (1962) *The Shell Country Book*. London: Pheonix.

Hardy, T. (1998) *Everyman's Poetry*. London: Orion.

Hudson, W.H. (1921) *A Traveller in Little Things*. Downloaded from: www.gutenberg.org.

Hudson, W.H. (1928) *Hampshire Days*. London: New Readers Library.

Hudson, W.H. (1951) *A Hind in Richmond Park*. London: J. M. Dent & Sons.

Hughes, T. (2003) *Ted Hughes: Collected Poems*. London: Faber & Faber.

Hughes, T. And Heaney, S. (eds.) (1982) *The Rattle Bag: An Anthology of Poetry*. London: Faber & Faber.

Jefferies, R. (1948) *Chronicles of the Hedges and Other Essays*. London: Phoenix House.

Jefferies, R. (1883) *The Story of My Heart*. Downloaded from: www.richardjefferiessociety.co.uk

Jefferies, R. (1884*)* *The Life of Fields*. Downloaded from: www.richardjefferiessociety.co.uk

Jermyn, S.T. (1974) *Flora of Essex*. Colchester: Essex Wildlife Trust.

Johnston, R.F. and Janiga, M. (1995) *Feral Pigeons*. New York: Oxford University Press Inc.

Lovelock, J (1979) *Gaia: A new Look at Life on Earth*. Oxford: Oxford University Press.

Lovelock, J. (2000) *The Ages of Gaia*. Oxford: Oxford University Press.

Macbeth G. (ed.) (1965) *The Penguin Book of Animal Verse*. Harmondsworth: Penguin.

Macleod, R.D. (1954) *Key to the Names of British Birds*. London: Sir Isaac Pitman and Sons.

Macleod, R.D. (1959) *Key to the Names of British Butterflies and Moths*. London: Sir Isaac Pitman and Sons.

Mills, A. D. (1991) *A Dictionary of English Place-names*. Oxford: Oxford University Press.

Mitchell, A. (1996) *Alan Mitchell's Trees of Britain*. London: Harper Collins

Murphy, P. (1996) Environmental Archaeology in Essex, in: Bedwin, O. (ed) *The Archaeology of Essex: Proceedings of the Writtle Conference*. Chelmsford: Essex County Council.

Murton, R.J. and Westwood, N.K. (1966) The foods of the Rock Dove and Feral Pigeon., *Bird Study*, 13:130-146.

Owen, J. (1991) *The ecology of a garden: The first fifteen years*. Cambridge: Cambridge University Press.

Pigeon Control Resource Centre website: www.pigeoncontrolresourcecentre.org

Rackham, O. (2000) *The Illustrated History of the Countryside*. London: Seven Dials.

Rainforest Concern website: www.rainforestconcern.org.

Rose, F. (revised and expanded by O'Reilly, C.) (2006) *The Wildflower Key*. London: Penguin Books.

Royal Society for the Protection of Birds website: www.rspb.org.uk

Thomas, E. (2002) *In Pursuit of Spring*. Holt: Laurel Books.

Thomas, E. (2009) *One Green Field*. London: Penguin.

Thomas, E. (2011) Edward Thomas Selected Poems. London: Faber & Faber.

Wainwright, A. (1987) *A Pennine Journey: The Story of a long Walk in 1938*. Harmondsworth: Penguin.

Warne. K. (2007) Blue Haven, *National Geographic*, April 2007.

Watson, E.L.G. (1992) *The Mystery of Physical Life*. Edinburgh: Floris Books.

Wilson, E.O. (1984) *Biophilia: The human bond with other species*. Cambridge, Massachusetts: Harvard University Press.

Species mentioned in text

Plants

Alder	*Alnus glutinosa*
Anemone, Wood	*Anemone nemorosa*
Apple, Crab	*Malus sylvestris*
Archangel, Yellow	*Lamiastrum galeobdolon*
Ash	*Fraxinus excelsior*
Avens, Wood	*Geum urbanum*
Beech	*Fagus sylvatica*
Bellflower, Clustered	*Campanula glomerata*
Bent sp.	*Agrostis* sp.
Birch	*Betula sp.*
Bird's-foot Trefoil, Common	*Lotus corniculatus*
Bird's-foot Trefoil, Greater	*Lotus pedunculatus*
Blackthorn	*Prunus spinosa*
Burnet-saxifrage, Greater	*Pimpinella major*
Bramble	*Rubus fruticosus*
Brome spp.	*Bromus* and *Bromopsis* spp.
Buttercup	*Ranunculus* spp.
Campion, Red	*Silene dioica*
Chaste Tree	*Vitex agnus-castus*
Cherry, Wild	*Prunus avium*
Chestnut, Horse	*Aesculus hippocastanum*
Clover, Red	*Trifolium pratense*
Clover, Sulphur	*Trifolium ochroleucon*
Clover, White	*Trifolium repens*

Columbine	*Aquilegia vulgaris*
Comfrey, Russian	*Symphytum × uplandicum*
Cow-wheat, Common	*Melampyrum pratense*
Cow-wheat, Crested	*Melampyrum cristatum*
Crane's-bill spp.	*Geranium* spp.
Cuckoo-pint	*Arum maculatum*
Daisy, Ox-eye	*Leucanthemum vulgare*
Dandelion	*Taraxacum* sp.
Dead-nettle sp.	*Lamium* sp.
Dock sp.	*Rumex* sp.
Elder	*Sambucus nigra*
Fern, Hard	*Polystichum aculeatum*
Fleabane	*Pulicaria dysenterica*
Forget-me-not, Water	*Myosotis scorpioides*
Foxglove	*Digitalis purpurea*
Furze	*Ulex europaeus*
Gorse	*Ulex europaeus*
Ground Ivy	*Glechoma hederacea*
Hawk's-beard sp.	*Crepis* sp.
Hawthorn	*Crataegus monogyna*
Hawthorn, Midland	*Crataegus laevigata*
Hazel	*Corylus avellana*
Hedge-garlic	*Alliaria petiolata*
Hellebore, Stinking	*Helleborus foetidus*
Hemp-agrimony	*Eupatorium cannabinum*
Herb-robert	*Geranium robertianum*
Hogweed	*Heracleum sphondylium*
Holly	*Ilex aquifolium*
Honeysuckle	*Lonicera periclymenum*
Hornbeam	*Carpinus betulus*
Iris, Yellow	*Iris pseudacorus*
Knapweed sp.	*Centaurea* sp.
Lime	*Tilia* sp.
Ling	*Calluna vulgaris*
Maple, Field	*Acer campestre*

Meadow-grass sp.	*Poa* sp.
Meadowsweet	*Filipendula ulmaria*
Melick, Wood	*Melica uniflora*
Mistletoe	*Viscum ablum*
Nettle, Stinging	*Urtica dioica*
Oak sp.	*Quercus* sp.
Oak, English	*Quercus robur*
Orchid, Common Spotted	*Dactylorhiza fuchsii*
Orchid, Green-winged	*Anacamptis morio*
Orchid, Lady	*Orchis purpurea*
Orchid, Pyramidal	*Anacamptis pyramidalis*
Pine, Calabrian	*Pinus brutia*
Plantain, Greater	*Plantago major*
Plantain, Ribwort	*Plantago lanceolata*
Rose, Dog	*Rosa canina*
Rowan	*Sorbus aucuparia*
Sallow	*Salix cinerea*
Sedge, Wood	*Carex sylvatica*
Service, Wild	*Sorbus torminalis*
Sorrel, Common	*Rumex acetosa*
Spurge, Mediterranean	*Euphorbia characias*
Thistle, Syrian	*Notobasis syriaca*
Vetch, Kidney	*Anthyllis vulneraria*
Vetch, Tufted	*Vicia cracca*
Vetchling, Grass	*Lathyrus nissolia*
Water-lily, Yellow	*Nuphar lutea*
Water-plantain	*Alisma plantago-aquatica*
Wayfaring Tree	*Viburnum lantana*
Willow	*Salix* sp.
Willow, Goat	*Salix caprea*
Willowherb sp.	*Epilobium* sp.
Woodruff, Sweet	*Galium odoratum*
Woodrush, Great	*Luzula sylvatica*
Woodrush, Hairy	*Luzula pilosa*
Yarrow	*Achillea millefolium*

Yellow-wort — *Blackstonia perfoliata*
Yew — *Taxus baccata*

Insects

Bristletails (*Thysanura*)
Silverfish — *Lepisma saccharina*

Mayflies (*Ephemeroptera*)

Dragonflies and Damselflies (*Odonata*)
Darter, Ruddy — *Sympetrum sanguineum*
Demoiselle, Banded — *Calopteryx splendens*
Dragonfly, Gold-ringed — *Cordulegaster boltonii*
Skimmer, Small — *Orthetrum taeniolatum*
Skimmer, Southern — *Orthetrum brunneum*
Spreadwing, Eastern Willow — *Lestes parvidens*

Crickets and Grasshoppers (*Orthoptera*)
Bush-cricket, Dark — *Pholidoptera griseoaptera*
Bush-cricket, Great Green — *Tettigonia viridissima*
Bush-cricket, Oak — *Meconema thalassinum*
Bush-cricket, Speckled — *Leptophyes punctatissima*
Grasshopper, Field — *Chorthippus brunneus*
Grasshopper, Meadow — *Chorthippus parallelus*
Grasshopper, Red-winged — *Oedipoda germanica*

True Bugs (*Hemiptera*)
Cicada — *Tibicen plebejus*
Greenfly — Superfamily Aphidoidea
Psyllid, Apple — *Psylla mali*
Shield Bug, Gorse — *Piezodorus lituratus*

Butterflies and Moths (*Lepidoptera*)

Admiral, White	*Limenitis Camilla*
Blue, Adonis	*Polyommatus bellargus*
Blue, Chalkhill	*Polyommatus coridon*
Blue, Holly	*Celastrina argiolus*
Blue, Small	*Cupido minimus*
Brown, Large Wall	*Lasiommata maera*
Brown, Meadow	*Maniola jurtina*
Cardinal	*Argynnis pandora*
Comma	*Polygonia c-album*
Copper, Small	*Lycaena phlaeas*
Fritillary, Heath	*Melitaea athalia*
Fritillary, Silver-washed	*Argynnis paphia*
Grayling, Great Banded	*Brintesia circe*
Hairsteak, Purple	*Neozephyrus quercus*
Monarch	*Danaus plexippus,*
Peacock	*Aglais io*
Ringlet	*Aphantopus hyperantus*
Skipper, Silver-spotted	*Hesperia comma*
Skipper, Small	*Thymelicus sylvestris*
Speckled Wood	*Pararge aegeria*
Tortoiseshell, Small	*Aglais urticae*
White, Green-veined	*Pieris napi*
White, Small	*Pieris rapae*

Burnet Companion	*Euclidia glyphica*
Burnet, Narrow-bordered 5-spot	*Zygaena lonicerae*
Burnet, Six-spot	*Zygaena filipendulae*
Carpet, Chalk	*Scotopteryx bipunctaria*
Case-bearer, Apple and Plum	*Coleophora spinella*
Clouded Silver	*Lomographa temerata*
Dart, Garden	*Euxoa nigricans*
Figure of Eight	*Diloba caeruleocephala*
Fox	*Macrothylacia rubi*
Heart and Club	*Agrotis clavis*

Heath, Common	*Ematurga atomaria*
Heath, Latticed	*Chiasmia clathrata*
Mother Shipton	*Callistege mi*
Pug, Narrow-winged	*Eupithecia nanata*
Rustic, Autumnal	*Eugnorisma glareosa*
Shaded Broad-bar	*Scotopteryx chenopodiata*
Short-cloaked	*Nola cucullatella*
Golden Pigmy	*Stigmella aurella*
Tiger spp.	*Arctia* spp.

Caddis Flies (Trichoptera)

True Flies (*Diptera*)

Agromyza nana

Bee-fly	*Bombylius major*
Cranefly	*Tipula* sp.
Dronefly	*Eristalis tenax*
Fly, Empid	*Empis tessellata*
Hoverfly, Bumblebee	*Volucella bombylans*

Melanostoma sp.
Platycheirus sp.
Volucella zonaria

Ants, Bees and Wasps (*Hymenoptera*)

Anthophora plumipes

Bee, Leaf-cutter	*Megachile* sp.
Bee, Nomad	*Nomada* sp.
Bumblebee, Buff-tailed	*Bombus terrestris*
Bumblebee, Early-nesting	*Bombus pratorum*
Bumblebee, Forest Cuckoo	*Bombus sylvestris*
Bumblebee, Red-tailed	*Bombus lapidarius*
Bumblebee, Red-tailed Cuckoo	*Bombus rupestris*
Bumblebee, Southern Cuckoo	*Bombus vestalis*
Bumblebee, Tree	*Bombus hypnorum*
Bumblebee, White-tailed	*Bombus lucorum*

Carder Bee, Brown-banded   *Bombus humilis*
Carder Bee, Common   *Bombus pascuorum*
Carder Bee, Shrill   *Bombus sylvarum*
Coelioxyx sp.
Hornet, Oriental   *Vespa orientalis*
Stelis sp.
Wasp, Digger sp.   Family Sphecidae
Wasp, Ichneumon sp.   Family Ichneumonidae

Beetles (*Coleoptera*)
Beetle, Rove sp.   Family Staphylinidae
Beetle, Soldier   *Rhagonycha fulva*
Beetle. Sailor   *Cantharis rustica*
Glow-worm   *Lampyris noctiluca*
Weevil, Pea   *Sitona lineatus*

Arachnids

Spiders (*Araneae*)
Misumena vatia
Spider, Daddy-long-legs   *Pholcus phalangioides*
Spider, House   *Tegenaria* sp.
Spider, Wolf   *Pardosa* sp.

Birds
Bittern   *Botaurus stellaris*
Blackbird   *Turdus merula*
Blackcap   *Sylvia atricapilla*
Buzzard   *Buteo buteo*
Chaffinch   *Fringilla coelebs*
Chiffchaff   *Pyhlloscopus collybita*
Coot   *Fulica atra*
Cormorant   *Phalacrocorax carbo*
Crow, Carrion   *Corvus corone*
Curlew   *Numenius arquata*

Dipper	*Cinclus cinclus*
Dove, Rock	*Columba livia*
Dunlin	*Calidris alpina*
Eagle, Golden	*Aquila chrysaetos*
Eider	*Somateria mollissima*
Fieldfare	*Turdus pilaris*
Flycatcher, Pied	*Ficedula hypoleuca*
Flycatcher, Spotted	*Muscicapa striata*
Garganey	*Anas querquedula*
Goose, Canada	*Branta canadensis*
Grebe, Great Crested	*Podiceps cristatus*
Gull, Black-headed	*Larus ridibundus*
Harrier, Marsh	*Circus aeruginosus*
Hobby	*Falco subbuteo*
Jay	*Garrulus glandarius*
Kestrel	*Falco tinnunculus*
Kingfisher	*Alcedo atthis*
Lapwing	*Vanellus vanellus*
Linnet	*Carduelis cannabina*
Magpie	*Pica pica*
Mallard	*Anas platyrhynchos*
Merlin	*Falco columbarius*
Moorhen	*Gallinula chloropus*
Nightingale	*Luscinia megarhynchos*
Nuthatch, European	*Sitta europaea*
Nuthatch, Krüper's	*Sitta krueperi*
Oystercatcher	*Haematopus ostralegus*
Parakeet, Ring-necked	*Psittacula krameri*
Peregrine	*Falco peregrinus*
Phalarope, Grey/Red	*Phalaropus fulicarius*
Pigeon, Feral	*Columba livia f. domestica*
Pipit sp.	*Anthus* sp.
Raven	*Corvus corax*
Robin	*Erithacus rubecula*
Rook	*Corvus frugilegus*

Shearwater, Mediterranean	*Puffinus yelkouan*
Snipe	*Gallinago gallinago*
Sparrowhawk	*Accipiter nisus*
Swift	*Apus apus*
Tern, Whiskered	*Chlidonias hybridus*
Tit, Blue	*Cyanistes caeruleus*
Tit, Coal	*Periparus ater*
Tit, Great	*Parus major*
Tit, Long-tailed	*Aegithalos caudatus*
Treecreeper	*Certhia familiaris*
Treecreeper, Short-toed	*Certhia brachydactyla*
Warbler, Grasshopper	*Locustella naevia*
Warbler, Willow	*Phylloscopus trochilus*
Warbler, Wood	*Phylloscopus sibilatrix*
Wheatear	*Oenanthe oenanthe*
Whitethroat	*Sylvia communis*
Woodpecker, Great Spotted	*Dendrocopos major*
Woodpigeon	*Columba palumbus*

Mammals

Cat, Wild	*Felis silvestris*
Deer, Red	*Cervus elaphus*
Deer, Roe	*Capreolus capreolus*
Dolphin, Bottle-nosed	*Tursiops truncatus*
Fox, Red	*Vulpes vulpes*
Marten, Pine	*Martes martes*
Mouse, Wood	*Apodemus sylvaticus*
Otter	*Lutra lutra*
Rabbit	*Lepus europaeus*
Seal, Common	*Phoca vitulina*
Seal, Grey	*Halichoeris grypus*
Vole, Bank	*Clethrionomys glareolus*
Vole (Rat), Water	*Arvicola terrestris*
Weasel	*Mustela nivalis*
Wolf	*Canis lupus*

Reptiles and Amphibians
Adder	*Vipera berus*
Agama, Starred	*Laudakia stellio*
Frog, Marsh	*Rana ridibunda*
Lizard, Common	*Lacerta vivipara*
Lizard, Danford's	*Lacerta anatolica*

Fish
Trout (Brown)	*Salmo trutta*
Tuna, Bluefin	*Thunnus thynnus*

Other Nature Books by Brambleby Books

Winging it – Birding for Low-flyers
Andrew Fallan
ISBN 9780955392856

The Ruffled Edge – Notes from a Nature Warden
Pete Howard
ISBN 9781908241061

Bird Words – Poetic images of wild birds
Hugh D. Loxdale
ISBN 9780954334734

Scilly Birding – Joining the madding crowd
Simon Davey
ISBN 9781908241177

Sheer Cliffs and Shearwaters – A Skomer Island Journal
Richard Kipling
ISBN 9781908241214

Never a dull Moment – A naturalist's view of British wildlife
Ross Gardner
ISBN 9780955392870

Garden Photo Shoot – A photographer's Year Book of Garden Wildlife
John Thurlbourn
ISBN 9780955392832

Walking with Birds
Colin Whittle
ISBN 9781908241351

www.bramblebybooks.co.uk